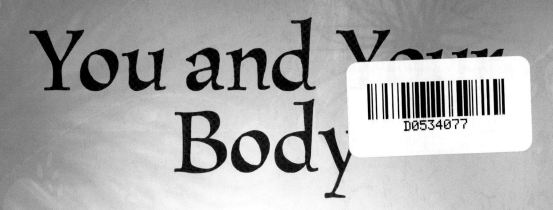

You and Your Body

Susan Meredith, Kate Needham and Mike Unwin

Designed by Lindy Dark and Non Figg

Illustrated by Kuo Kang Chen, Colin King, Annabel Spenceley, Sue Stitt and Peter Wingham

Consultants: Cynthia Beverton, Dr Michael Hitchcock, Dr John Kesby, Valerie Micheau, Indu Patel, Dr Frank Slattery and Dr Kevan Thorley

Contents

What's Inside You?

Contents

What does your body do?

Your body is made of masses of different parts. Each part has its own important job to do. All the parts have to work properly together to keep you alive and healthy.

Even when you are doing something quite straightforward, like playing, lots and lots of complicated things are going on inside your body.

Your brain tells all the different parts of you what to do.

You listen to the sounds around you using your ears. Your ears also help you to keep your balance.

Your muscles make you move so you can throw and catch a ball.

Your eyes work hard watching the ball carefully.

Sometimes your muscles start to ache. This tells you it is time for a rest.

Feelers in your body, called nerves, tell you what your body is doing and what is happening to it.

Your mouth shapes sounds into words when you talk.

If you fall and graze your knee, a few drops of blood may spill out but your body soon heals itself.

Your body has a framework of bones which helps it to keep its shape whatever you are doing.

If you have been sweating a lot, you may feel thirsty.

If it is hot, you may sweat and go red in the face. This is really your body's way of cooling you down.

You can smell the flowers with your nose.

Your food and drink are travelling through your body. You may need to go to the toilet to get rid of some waste.

You may feel your heart beating in your chest. It is pumping blood around your body to give you energy.

You breathe hard to give your body extra energy.

Babies are exploring and learning all the time.

You are growing very, very gradually all the time.

What colour are you inside?

In this book your insides are shown in all different colours so you can see the different parts clearly.

Most of your insides are really a brownish-red colour a bit like meat.

3

Eating

Your body needs food and drink to keep working properly.

Using your teeth

You use your teeth to make your food small enough to swallow. Your front teeth are a different shape from your back teeth. Can you feel the difference with your tongue?

Two sets of teeth

Your first set of teeth are called milk teeth because they grow when you are a baby. There are 20 of these.

The milk tooth will eventually fall out as the adult tooth grows up underneath it.

There are 32 teeth in a full adult set. Nobody really knows why people grow two sets of teeth.

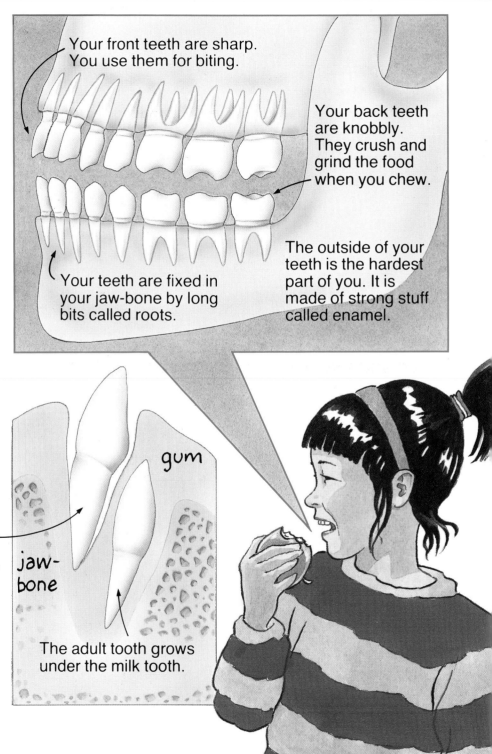

Your front teeth are sharp. You use them for biting.

Your back teeth are knobbly. They crush and grind the food when you chew.

Your teeth are fixed in your jaw-bone by long bits called roots.

The outside of your teeth is the hardest part of you. It is made of strong stuff called enamel.

gum

jaw-bone

The adult tooth grows under the milk tooth.

4

Food

Different foods do different jobs in your body. You need to eat small amounts of lots of different kinds of food to stay really healthy.

Potatoes, rice, pasta, bread and sweet food give you energy.

Milk, cheese and yogurt make your bones and teeth strong.

Foods such as meat, fish and eggs make you grow and help to repair your body.

Fruit and vegetables have vitamins in them. These keep your body working efficiently.

Cleaning teeth

It is important to clean your teeth well, especially last thing at night.

Tiny bits of food and drink stick to your teeth even though you cannot feel them.

If the bits are left on your teeth, chemicals called acids are made. The acids make holes in your teeth.

Where your food goes

Before your body can use the food you eat, it has to be changed into microscopically tiny bits inside you. It has to be so small it can get into your blood. This is called digestion.

Digesting food

Your food is digested as it goes through a long tube winding from your mouth to your bottom. The tube has different parts, shown here.

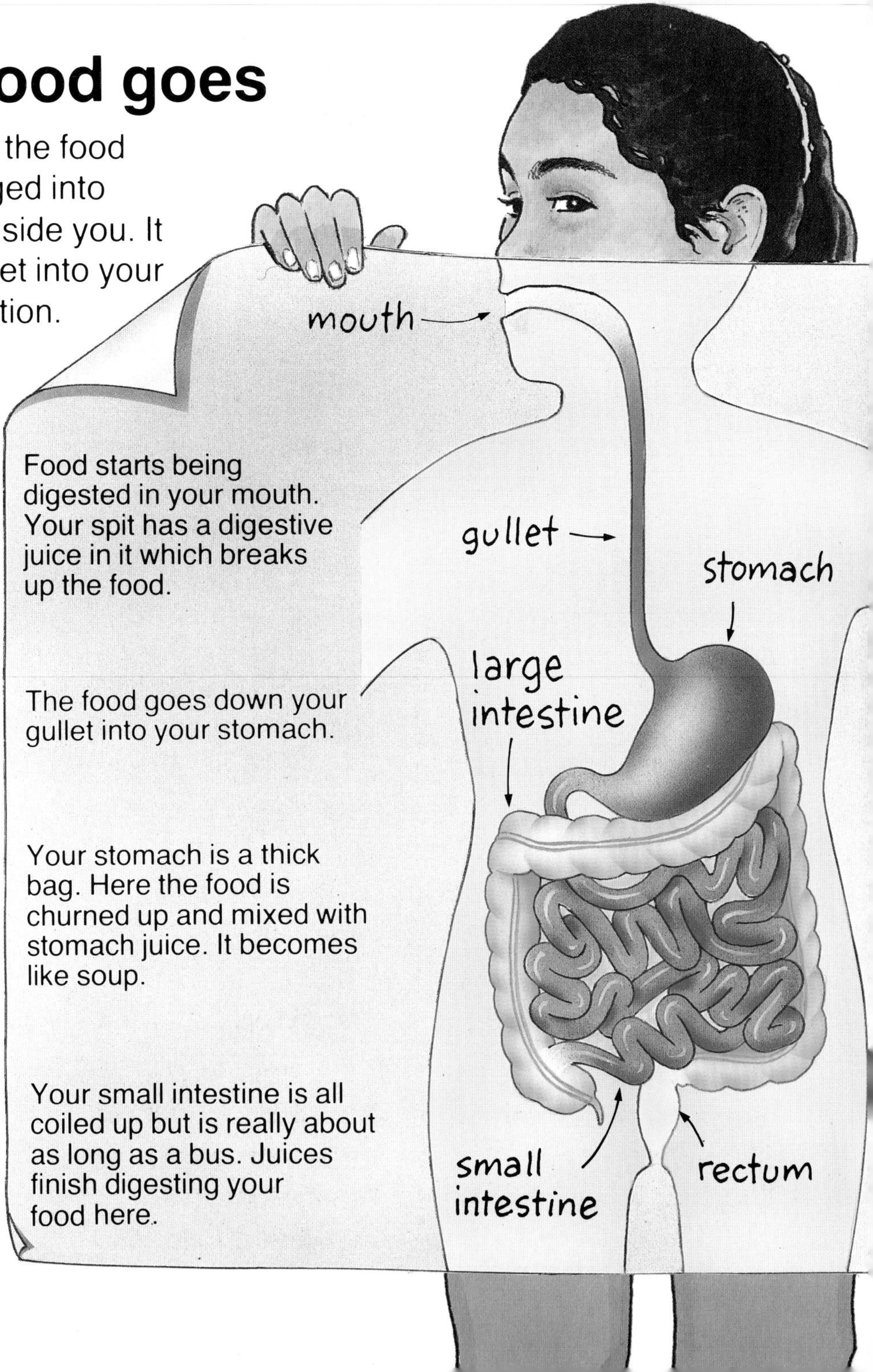

Three-day journey

A meal stays in your stomach for about four hours. It takes about three days to travel right through you.

Food starts being digested in your mouth. Your spit has a digestive juice in it which breaks up the food.

The food goes down your gullet into your stomach.

Your stomach is a thick bag. Here the food is churned up and mixed with stomach juice. It becomes like soup.

Your small intestine is all coiled up but is really about as long as a bus. Juices finish digesting your food here.

mouth

gullet

stomach

large intestine

small intestine

rectum

6

The digested food seeps through the thin walls of your small intestine into your blood.

digested food   intestine wall

blood

Your blood carries food all around your body.

Water from your food and drink goes into your blood through the walls of your large intestine.

Some bits of food cannot be digested. You push them out of your rectum when you go to the toilet.

Waste water

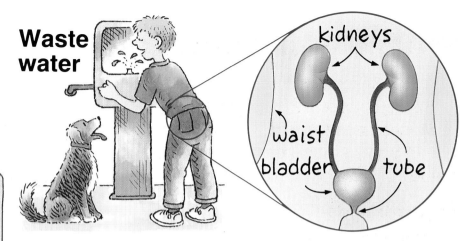

kidneys

waist

bladder   tube

Any water that your body does not need is turned into urine (wee) in your kidneys. These are in your back.

Urine is stored in a bag called a bladder. You can feel your bladder getting full when you need to go to the toilet.

How food moves along

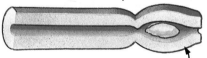

food

Muscles squeeze here.

Food is pushed along.

Food does not slide through you. It is squeezed along by muscles in your digestive tube.

Tummy rumbles

The sound you hear when your tummy rumbles is food and air being squeezed along your digestive tube.

7

Why do you breathe?

Before your body can use the energy which is in your food, the food has to be mixed with oxygen. Oxygen is a gas which is in the air all around you. When you breathe in, you take oxygen into your body.

How you breathe

The air you breathe is sucked up your nose or into your mouth, down your windpipe and into your lungs.

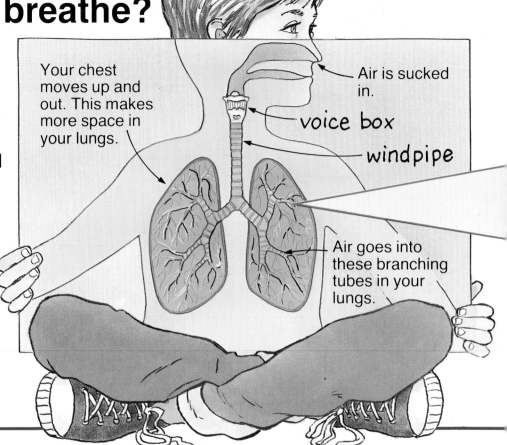

Your chest moves up and out. This makes more space in your lungs.

Air is sucked in.

voice box

windpipe

Air goes into these branching tubes in your lungs.

Voice box

mmm..

The lumpy bit in your neck is your voice box. It is at the top of your windpipe.

Can you feel a sort of wobbling there when you say a loud "mmm" sound?

When you breathe out, air goes through some stretchy cords in your voice box. If there is enough air, the cords wobble like guitar strings when you play them. This makes sounds. Your mouth shapes the sounds into words.

At the ends of the tubes in your lungs are bunches of air sacs. These fill up with air like balloons.

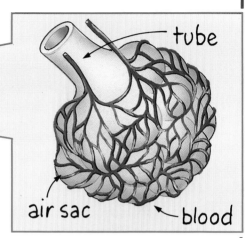

tube

air sac — blood

Oxygen seeps through the air sac walls into your blood.

Your blood carries the oxygen around your body. The oxygen mixes with digested food to give you energy.

A waste gas called carbon dioxide is made. Your blood carries this back to your lungs.

When you breathe out, air is squeezed out of your lungs. The air has carbon dioxide in it.

Your chest moves in so there is less space in your lungs.

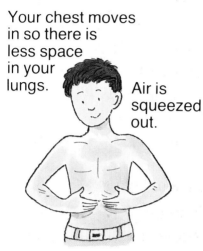

Air is squeezed out.

Can you feel your chest moving in and out as you breathe?

Hiccups

The sound is the cords in your voice box closing suddenly.

There is a large muscle below your lungs. This moves up and down as you breathe. Sometimes it gets out of control and you get hiccups.

Choking on food

Your windpipe is very close to your gullet.

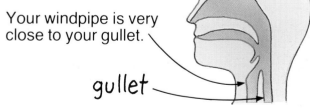

gullet

When you choke on your food, you say it has "gone down the wrong way". This is true. It has gone down your windpipe instead of your gullet.

9

What is blood for?

The main job of your blood is to carry food and oxygen to all parts of your body. It also collects waste, such as carbon dioxide, so you can get rid of it.

How blood moves

Your blood is flowing around your body all the time in thin tubes called blood vessels. It is kept moving by your heart.

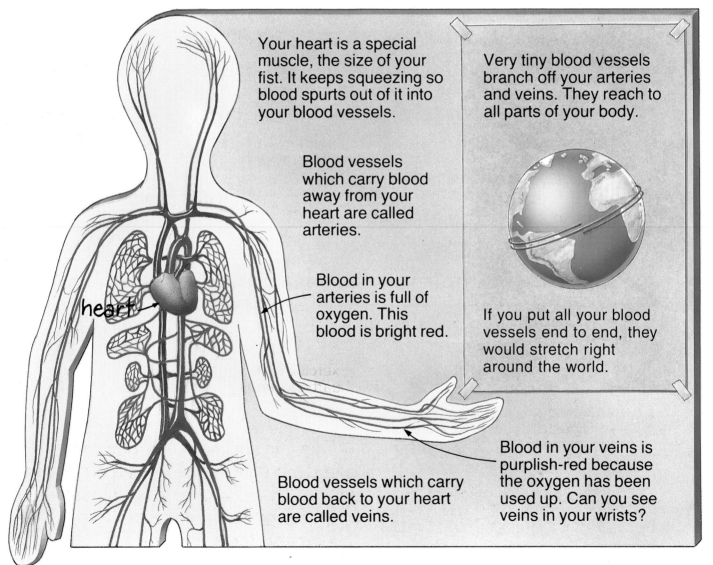

Your heart is a special muscle, the size of your fist. It keeps squeezing so blood spurts out of it into your blood vessels.

Blood vessels which carry blood away from your heart are called arteries.

Blood in your arteries is full of oxygen. This blood is bright red.

heart→

Very tiny blood vessels branch off your arteries and veins. They reach to all parts of your body.

If you put all your blood vessels end to end, they would stretch right around the world.

Blood vessels which carry blood back to your heart are called veins.

Blood in your veins is purplish-red because the oxygen has been used up. Can you see veins in your wrists?

What is blood?

If you looked at a drop of blood through a microscope, you would see that it had lots of bits floating in it.

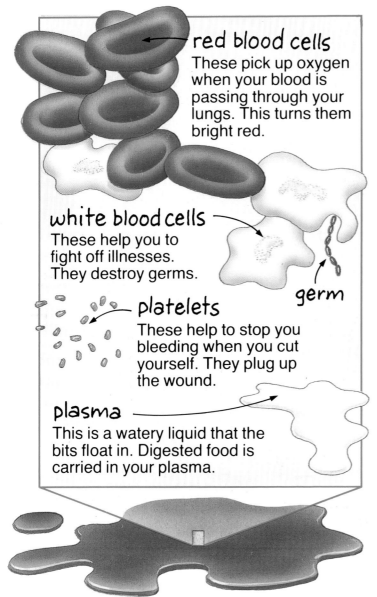

red blood cells
These pick up oxygen when your blood is passing through your lungs. This turns them bright red.

white blood cells
These help you to fight off illnesses. They destroy germs.

germ

platelets
These help to stop you bleeding when you cut yourself. They plug up the wound.

plasma
This is a watery liquid that the bits float in. Digested food is carried in your plasma.

Heartbeats

An adult's heart beats about 70 times a minute; a child's beats 80 to 100 times.

You can hear people's hearts beating. The sound is made by valves. These are like gates in the heart. They slam shut after each spurt of blood has gone through.

Being energetic

Exercise makes your heart and lungs stronger.

When you are being energetic, you need more food and oxygen to keep going. That is why your heart beats faster and harder, and why you breathe faster and deeper.

Your skin

Your skin is like a bag which holds your body together. But it has other jobs too. It works all the time to protect you from the outside world.

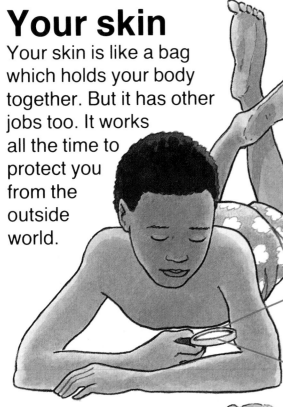

Your skin is only about 2mm ($\frac{1}{12}$ inch) thick over most of your body. This picture makes it look much thicker so you can see inside it.

Your hairs grow out of deep pits. Can you see that you have hair on your body as well as on your head?

Blood vessels bring food and oxygen to your skin.

Red in the face

More blood in your skin makes you look red.

When you get hot, the blood vessels in your skin widen. This means that more blood flows near the surface and makes you look red. The air cools down the blood, and you.

Goosepimples

When furry animals get goosepimples, air gets trapped in their fur and helps to keep them warm.

When you are cold, your hair muscles tighten up and make the hair on your body stand on end. This is what makes goosepimples. Goosepimples are not much use to humans.

As your hair grows, the ends get so far away from your blood that they die.

The skin you can see is dead because it is too far from your blood vessels.

Sweat comes out of holes called pores. The air cools you down as it dries the sweat on your skin.

Your hairs have muscles attached to them.

Your dead skin gets worn away. New skin grows up from below to replace it.

This is a store of fat, which comes from your food. Fat helps to keep you warm and can be used for energy.

Your hair and skin are coated with oil, which is made here. The oil helps stop water soaking into your skin.

You feel things with nerve endings like this one.

Sweat is made in sweat glands. It is mainly water and salt. Have you ever tasted the salt?

Nails

Your nails are a bit like animals' claws. They are made of extremely hard skin.

Fair or dark?

Dark skin is better protected from the sun than fair skin.

Fair skin burns if it gets too much sun too quickly.

Some people's skin is darker than others': it has more of a dye called melanin in it.

More melanin is made in strong sunshine. This helps to protect you from the sun.

13

Messages from outside you

You tell what is happening outside you in five different ways: you see, hear, touch, taste and smell things. This is called using your senses.

How you see

Your eyes have special nerve endings in them which react to light. Light bounces off everything you see.

The light goes into your eyes through the black dot in the middle. The dot is really a hole called the pupil.

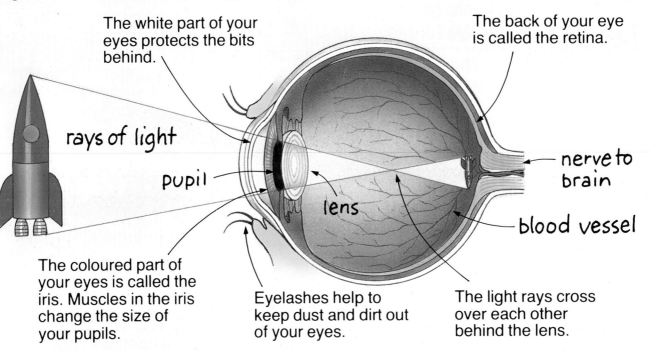

The white part of your eyes protects the bits behind.

The back of your eye is called the retina.

rays of light

pupil

lens

nerve to brain

blood vessel

The coloured part of your eyes is called the iris. Muscles in the iris change the size of your pupils.

Eyelashes help to keep dust and dirt out of your eyes.

The light rays cross over each other behind the lens.

Behind the pupil is a clear disc called a lens. This bends the light in a special way so that an upside-down picture of what you are looking at fits onto the back of your eye.

The nerve endings which react to light are on the back of your eye. They send the picture along a nerve to your brain. Your brain turns the picture back the right way up.

Tears

Tears are made under your top eyelids.

Nobody knows why people cry when they are upset.

Every time you blink, tears wash over your eyes and clean them.

Tears drain into your nose through the inside corners of your eyes.

Big or small pupils

You can watch your pupils changing size. Look at them first in a brightly lit place, then in a dimmer one.

When it is dark, your pupils get bigger to let in as much light as

possible. When it is bright, they shrink to protect your eye.

Wearing glasses

Glasses are lenses. They help the lenses in people's eyes to get the picture onto their retina properly.

Tasting

Your tongue has tiny spots called taste buds on it. These have nerve endings in them which sense different tastes.

Can you see the taste buds if you look at your tongue in a mirror?

Smelling

Nerve endings in your nose tell you about smells. Your senses of smell and taste often work together.

If your nose is blocked up with a cold, you can't taste as much.

15

Hearing and touching

How you hear

Sounds affect nerve endings right inside your ears.

The outside of your ears is like the big end of a funnel. It collects sounds.

The sounds go down a tube, called the ear canal. They hit some thin skin at the end, called the ear drum. The sounds make the ear drum wobble.

This part of your ear helps you to balance.

Nerve from ear to brain.

bone

Nerve endings and liquid are in here.

ear drum

This is the smallest bone in your body. It is about 3mm (1/8 inch) long and is called the stirrup.

ear canal

Tube from ear to nose.

outside of ear

When your ear drum wobbles, it makes three tiny bones wobble too. The bones pass the wobbling on further inside your ears.

The wobbling reaches deep inside your ears, where there is liquid and hairy nerve endings. The liquid moves about and pulls on the hairs.

The nerve endings send messages about the sounds to your brain.

16

Balancing

The balance part of your ear tells your brain what position your head is in.

When you know where your head is, you can adjust the rest of your body to balance.

Twitchy ears

Many animals can move their ears to search for sounds.

People cannot usually move their ears. Can you waggle yours a little bit if you concentrate really hard?

Touching and feeling

Nerve endings in your skin tell your brain whether things are hot, cold, rough, smooth, soft, hard, or painful.

You have lots and lots of nerve endings in your fingers, the soles of your feet, and in your lips and tongue.

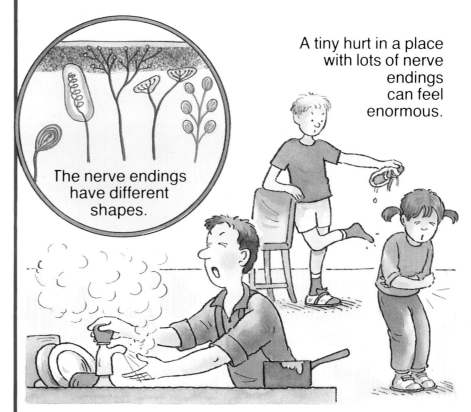

The nerve endings have different shapes.

A tiny hurt in a place with lots of nerve endings can feel enormous.

Pain is useful really. It warns you when something is wrong so you can save yourself from harm.

You have pain nerve endings deep inside your body as well as in your skin. These tell you when you are ill.

Inside your head

Your brain controls the rest of your body and makes sure that all the different parts of you work properly together. Your brain makes sense of what happens to you. It makes you able to think, learn and feel.

Brain and nerves

Your brain is connected to all parts of your body by nerves. These are a bit like telephone wires. Messages go to and from your brain along them.

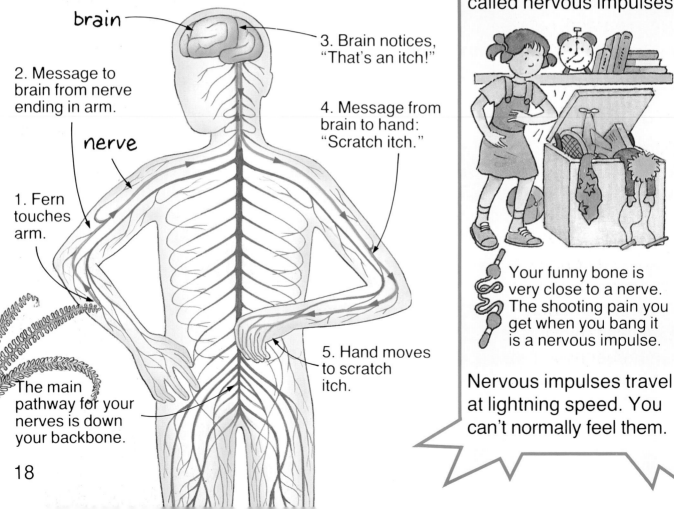

brain

2. Message to brain from nerve ending in arm.

nerve

1. Fern touches arm.

The main pathway for your nerves is down your backbone.

3. Brain notices, "That's an itch!"

4. Message from brain to hand: "Scratch itch."

5. Hand moves to scratch itch.

Body electricity

The messages which go along your nerves are electrical. They are called nervous impulses.

Your funny bone is very close to a nerve. The shooting pain you get when you bang it is a nervous impulse.

Nervous impulses travel at lightning speed. You can't normally feel them.

Learning

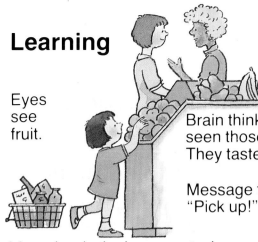

Eyes see fruit.

Brain thinks, "I've seen those before. They taste nice."

Message to hand: "Pick up!"

Your brain helps you to learn. It sorts out and stores all the messages it is sent. You work out what new messages mean by remembering old ones.

Sleeping

Dreaming may be a way of making sense of what has happened to you.

Your brain keeps working even when you are asleep. It makes sure your heart keeps beating and that you keep breathing and digesting food.

Parts of the brain

Different parts of your brain deal with different sorts of messages. There are some parts that nobody knows much about. They are probably to do with thinking, remembering and making decisions.

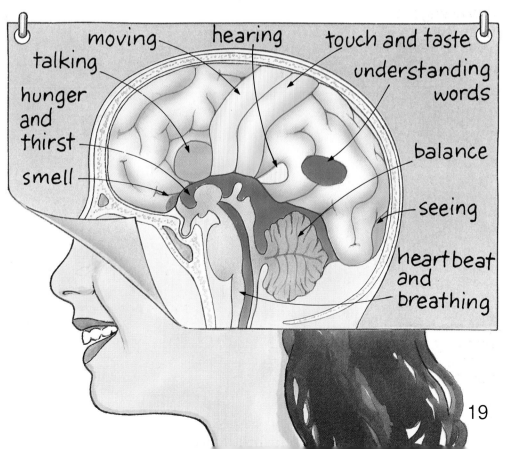

moving

hearing

touch and taste

talking

understanding words

hunger and thirst

smell

balance

seeing

heartbeat and breathing

19

What makes you move?

You are able to move because of the way your muscles, bones, brain and nerves all work together.

Your skeleton

Your skeleton has more than 200 bones. Besides helping you to move, your bones stop your body losing its shape and collapsing. Bones also protect other parts of your body.

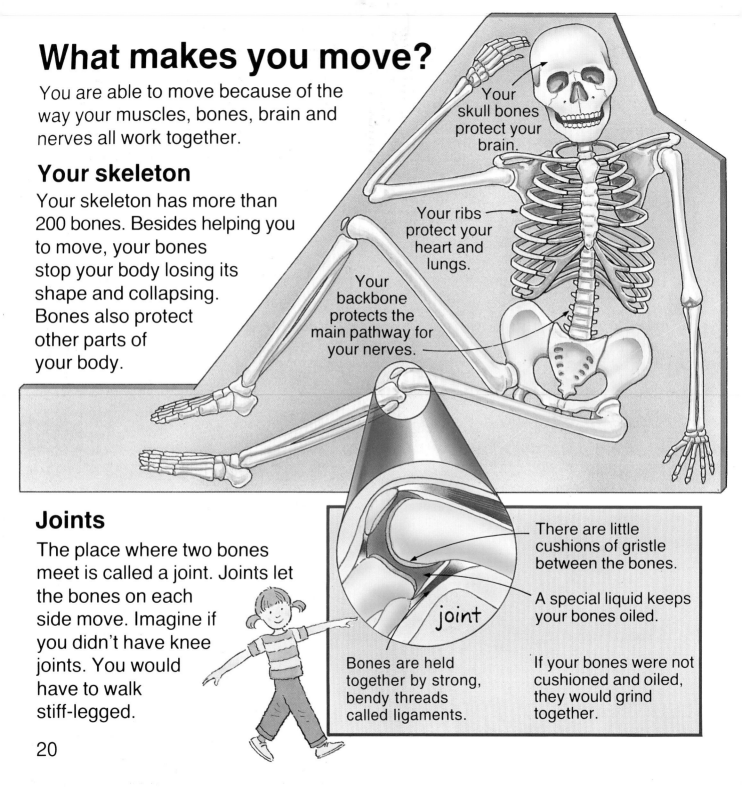

Your skull bones protect your brain.

Your ribs protect your heart and lungs.

Your backbone protects the main pathway for your nerves.

Joints

The place where two bones meet is called a joint. Joints let the bones on each side move. Imagine if you didn't have knee joints. You would have to walk stiff-legged.

joint

There are little cushions of gristle between the bones.

A special liquid keeps your bones oiled.

Bones are held together by strong, bendy threads called ligaments.

If your bones were not cushioned and oiled, they would grind together.

Muscles

All over your skeleton are stretchy muscles. They are fastened to your bones by strong cords called tendons.

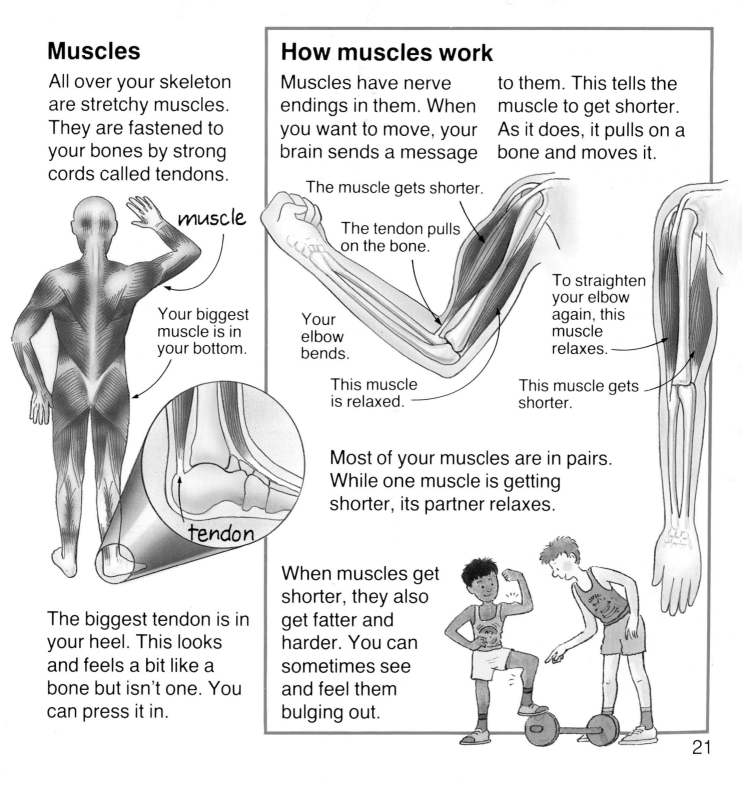

muscle

Your biggest muscle is in your bottom.

tendon

The biggest tendon is in your heel. This looks and feels a bit like a bone but isn't one. You can press it in.

How muscles work

Muscles have nerve endings in them. When you want to move, your brain sends a message to them. This tells the muscle to get shorter. As it does, it pulls on a bone and moves it.

The muscle gets shorter.

The tendon pulls on the bone.

Your elbow bends.

This muscle is relaxed.

To straighten your elbow again, this muscle relaxes.

This muscle gets shorter.

Most of your muscles are in pairs. While one muscle is getting shorter, its partner relaxes.

When muscles get shorter, they also get fatter and harder. You can sometimes see and feel them bulging out.

21

What is your body made of?

All the parts of your body are made of tiny living bits called cells. These are so small that you can only see them with a powerful microscope. You have millions of cells.

Below you can see what a group of skin cells looks like under a microscope.

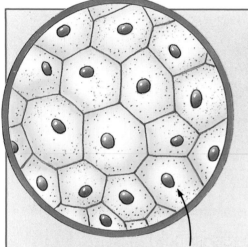

This part controls the way the cell works. It is called the nucleus.

Each of your cells is about two-thirds water. Food and oxygen mix together inside your cells to give you energy.

Chromosomes

The nucleus of each cell has special threads in it called chromosomes. These carry the instructions the cell needs to live, grow and work. Chromosomes are made of a chemical called DNA.

This picture shows part of a chromosome. The instructions for the cell are in code.

Different kinds of cells

Cells are different shapes and sizes depending on what job they have to do. Here are some examples.

nucleus

Messages travel along your nerves. Nerve cells are very long.

Nerve endings are like feelers.

Muscle cells are long and thin but they can get shorter and fatter. This makes you move.

Cells in your nose and windpipe have tiny hairs on them. These waft germs and dust away from your lungs.

Growing

Until you are about 18, your body keeps making more and more cells. This makes you get bigger.

New cells are made by a cell splitting in two.

a cell

The cell takes in goodness from food and swells up.

The cell divides in two.

Now there are two cells.

Body repairs

Even when you are grown up, your body has to make some new cells. These replace cells that wear out and die. Some cells live longer than others.

Cells in your intestines get worn away by food and only live for about six days.

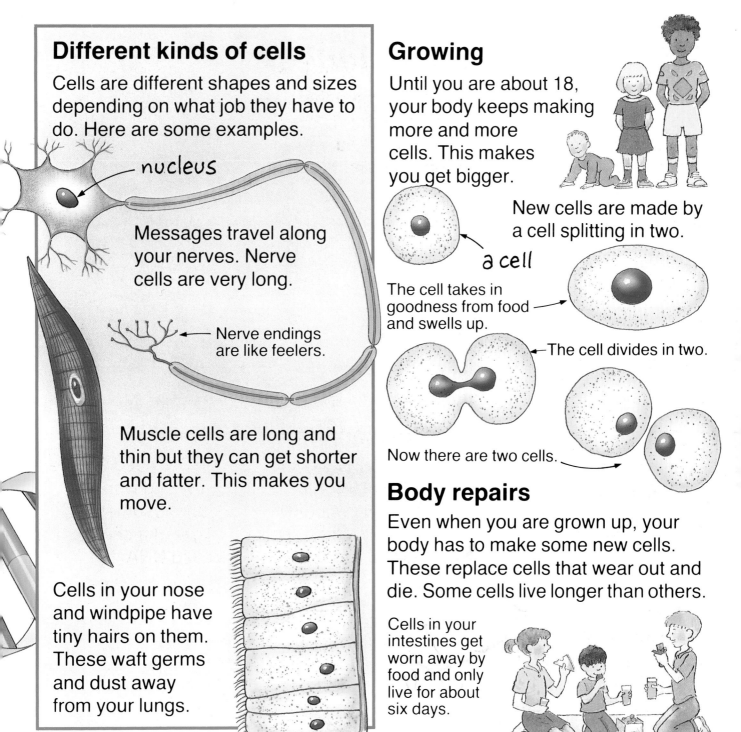

Amazing facts and figures

All together you have over 50 billion cells in your body. (A billion is a million million.)

All the nerves in your body, put end to end, would stretch for over 70km (43.5 miles).

Your brain needs so much oxygen that it uses almost one fifth of all the oxygen you breathe in.

You are born with about 350 bones in your body. As you grow up, many of these join together. Adults have just over 200 bones.

Average-sized adults have about 5 litres (10.5pt) of blood in their body. An average-sized seven year old has about 3 litres (6pt).

About 50 hairs drop out of your head every day even though you do not notice it. New hairs grow to take their place, though.

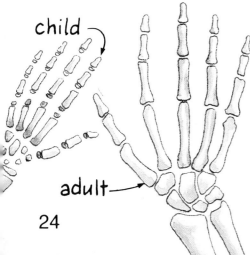

Why Do People Eat?

Contents

Why do you need food?

Your body is like a big machine that is always working. Even when you are asleep your heart is beating, your lungs are breathing and your brain is working. Food is the fuel which keeps all these things going. Without it you would slow down and eventually grind to a halt.

A bar of chocolate gives you enough energy to walk for an hour.

People need food just as cars need petrol.

An apple gives you enough energy to cycle for six minutes.

Growing big and strong

People sometimes say you have to eat things to grow big and strong. This is true because your whole body is made from good things in the food you eat.

Until you are about 18 your body is growing all the time.

Measure yourself each month to see how quickly you grow.

Sometimes when you haven't eaten you feel weak. This is because your body is running out of energy.

Children who don't get enough food stop growing. They become thin and weak and fall ill more easily.

Too much

If you eat more food than your body needs you store it as fat. This makes you heavy and slows you down.

Some people want to be big and heavy so they overeat on purpose. For example Japanese sumo wrestlers need to be heavy to fight.

Sumo wrestlers look like this.

On the mend

The good things in the food you eat help your body make repairs if it gets damaged. They also help you get better when you are ill.

When you cut yourself, the food you eat helps your body mend quickly.

Water

Water is what keeps your body moist and makes your blood flow around. Without it your body would dry out and stop working.

You can last several weeks without food but only a few days without water.

Loading and unloading bread from an oven is hot, thirsty work.

Shipwrecked sailors more often die of thirst than hunger, since they can't drink seawater.

People who work in hot places, such as a baker, need to drink more because they lose water when they sweat.

What is food made of?

Everything you eat is made up of lots of different things called nutrients. These are the good things that keep your body going. Proteins, fats and carbohydrates are all nutrients. Each one helps your body do a special job.

Protein

Proteins are like building blocks. Your body uses them to grow and repair itself. Different kinds of proteins help build up each part of your body.

Pregnant women need extra protein to help their baby grow.

A mother's milk has special proteins in it.

Proteins build up muscles and make your hair grow.

Teenagers use up lots of proteins because they are growing fast.

Meat, eggs, fish and cheese have lots of protein.

Carbohydrate

Carbohydrates give you energy. You need energy for everything you do such as running around, talking, thinking, even reading this book.

You get lots of energy from sweet things but it doesn't last very long. The energy you get from pasta, cereal or bread is better because it lasts longer.

Climbers often carry a bar of chocolate in case they need extra energy in an emergency.

Sporty people need carbohydrate for extra energy.

Bread, cereal, pasta and cakes have lots of carbohydrate.

Fat

Fat also gives you energy but unless your body needs it right away, it is stored in a layer around your body. This acts like an extra piece of clothing helping to keep you warm and protect you.

Butter, margarine and oil are almost all fat.

Fat stored on your bottom makes it more comfortable to sit on, like a little cushion.

29

What else is in food?

The food you eat also has tiny amounts of nutrients called vitamins and minerals which you need.

What do vitamins do?

Vitamins are like little workers which help other nutrients to do their jobs. There are about 20 different kinds. Most are named after letters of the alphabet.

The chart opposite shows what some vitamins do and where you find them.

A

Vitamin A helps you see in the dark.

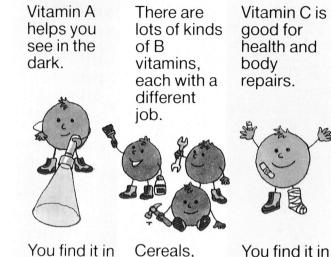

You find it in egg yolks, liver, full fat milk and carrots.

B

There are lots of kinds of B vitamins, each with a different job.

Cereals, dairy products and meat have B vitamins.

C

Vitamin C is good for health and body repairs.

You find it in fresh fruit and vegetables.

D

Vitamin D helps make your bones and teeth strong.

You get it from eggs, fish and butter.

Sailors used to get scurvy – a disease which stops wounds from healing. This is because they were at sea for months without any fresh vegetables or fruit and so no vitamin C.

Your body can make vitamin D itself using sunlight. People who live in less sunny countries need extra vitamin D from their food.

What are minerals?

Minerals are nutrients that plants get from soil and pass on to you. You need about 15 different ones such as salt, calcium and iron.

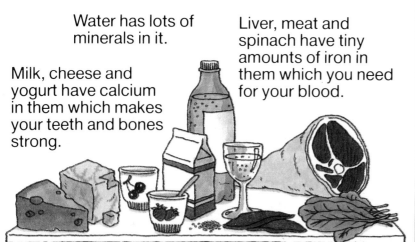

Water has lots of minerals in it.

Liver, meat and spinach have tiny amounts of iron in them which you need for your blood.

Milk, cheese and yogurt have calcium in them which makes your teeth and bones strong.

What is fibre?

Fibre is the tough bit of food that you don't digest. It helps carry food through you and takes waste out the other end.

Brown bread, cereals and vegetables have lots of fibre.

If you don't eat enough fibre you get constipated – this is when you can't go to the toilet for ages.

What do you eat?

Write down everything you ate and drank in your last main meal. Then see if you can find out which nutrients each thing had. Use the last two pages for help.

Roast chicken	—	protein
potatoes	—	carbohydrate vitamin C
peas and carrots	—	vitamin A vitamin C fibre
strawberries	—	vitamin C
ice cream	—	nothing particularly good

How many good things did you eat? Were there any you didn't get any of? Some things you eat, such as ice cream, may not have anything particularly good in them, see page 40.

Where does food go to?

When you eat, your food starts a long journey through your body which takes about three days. It travels through a tube called the alimentary canal which starts at your mouth and finishes at your bottom.

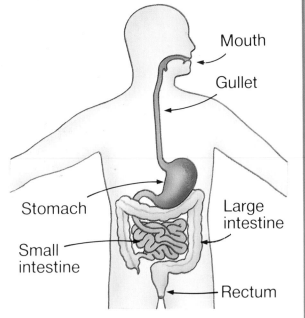

Mouth

Gullet

Stomach

Large intestine

Small intestine

Rectum

On the way, different parts of your body work on the food and add juices with chemicals in them. This breaks food into microscopically small pieces that can go into your blood. This journey is called digestion.

Food's journey

The road in this picture is like the alimentary canal, and the men show what happens to your food.

Your mouth

These men are like your teeth, cutting food into tiny pieces.

The water is like saliva. It makes food soft and mushy.

Your tongue rolls the food into a ball and pushes it into your gullet, like these men with brooms.

Your gullet

Then you swallow, and food is carried off from your mouth to continue its journey.

How long to chew?

The smaller food gets in your mouth, the easier it is for your stomach to work on. Tough meat or food with lots of fibre needs more chewing.

Eat a mouthful of apple. Then eat one of cheese.

See how many times you chew each one before you swallow .

What makes you choke?

Your gullet is next to your windpipe (the pipe you breath through). When you swallow, your windpipe closes to stop food from going into it.

If it doesn't close in time your food might go down the wrong way. This makes you choke which usually sends the food back up.

Wind-pipe → | Gullet

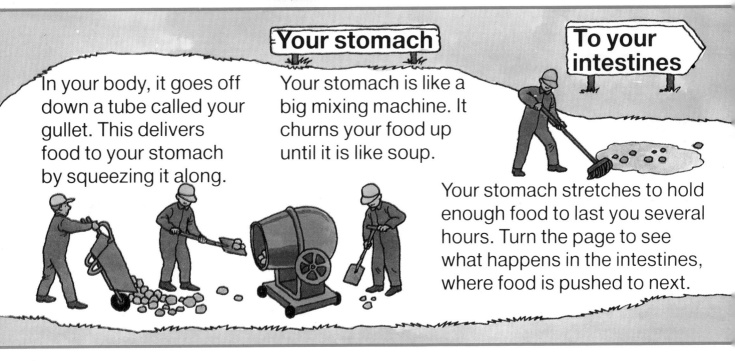

Your stomach

To your intestines

In your body, it goes off down a tube called your gullet. This delivers food to your stomach by squeezing it along.

Your stomach is like a big mixing machine. It churns your food up until it is like soup.

Your stomach stretches to hold enough food to last you several hours. Turn the page to see what happens in the intestines, where food is pushed to next.

Good things and waste

After about three hours, the soupy mixture in your stomach moves on to your intestines. There, all the good things in food are taken into the blood. The way it happens is called absorption. Waste moves on to leave your body. This is the longest part of food's journey.

Your small intestine

First the food arrives in your small intestine. This isn't really small at all, as it's a long tube all curled up.

How goodness is absorbed

The walls of your small intestine are so thin that the nutrients in your food can pass through them.

The nutrients go into your blood and are carried around your body.

Tiny folds stick out of the walls of the small intestine.

Blood flows all around the folds, ready to carry off nutrients.

goodness

waste

STAY

As the soupy mixture passes through it, more juices are added. Then nutrients are absorbed into your blood (the man's sign tells them to stay). The rest goes into your large intestine (the man's sign tells them they must go).

Your large intestine

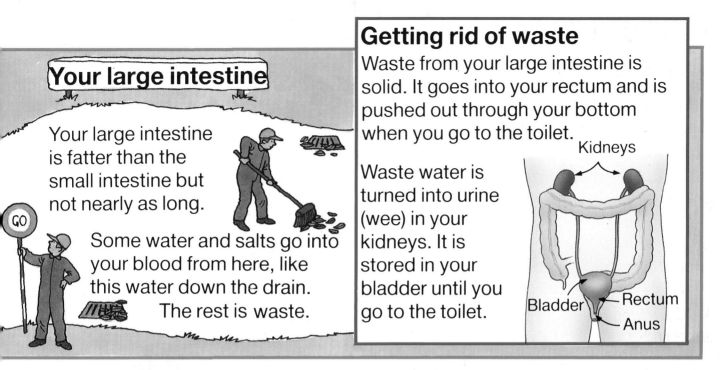

Your large intestine is fatter than the small intestine but not nearly as long.

Some water and salts go into your blood from here, like this water down the drain. The rest is waste.

Getting rid of waste

Waste from your large intestine is solid. It goes into your rectum and is pushed out through your bottom when you go to the toilet.

Waste water is turned into urine (wee) in your kidneys. It is stored in your bladder until you go to the toilet.

Kidneys

Bladder — Rectum — Anus

What makes you burp?

When you eat you often swallow air with your food. Sometimes your body sends the air back up through your mouth. This is a burp.

BURP!

Eating too fast makes you swallow lots of air and so you may burp.

Food poisoning

If you eat food that is bad, your body tries to get rid of it quickly.

Your stomach muscles may push it back up your gullet. This is when you are sick.

It may rush through you and come out the other end as diarrhoea.

35

Keeping food fresh

Your food is also food for tiny living things called microbes. These can make fresh food go bad after a few days. If you want food to keep you have to stop microbes from getting at it first. They like moisture, warmth and air, so food kept in cold, dry places with no air lasts longer.

No air

Today, lots of food is vacuum-packed. This is when all the air is sucked out of the packet. Bottles and cans have no air either. Can you hear air rushing back in when you open them?

VACUUM-PACKED PEANUTS

Keeping food cold

Cooling food slows microbes down; freezing it stops them altogether. Today, food can be kept in refrigerators or freezers until it is needed.

Cold cellars have been used to keep food for centuries.

The cold does not kill microbes, so you still have to eat food quickly when you defrost it.

Drying food

Drying food gets rid of all the moisture so microbes can't multiply.

Grapes are dried to make raisins, sultanas and currants.

Today, food can be freeze-dried. This is when it is frozen and dried at the same time to get rid of moisture. You add water when you eat it.

Astronauts use freeze-dried food as it's light and takes little room.

Heating food up

Cooking, sterilization and pasteurization are all ways of killing microbes by heat.

Sterilized food is heated to a very high temperature to kill all the microbes. It lasts a long time.

Vinegar in pickles

Sugar in jam

Salt in bacon

Food in cans and bottles is sterilized.

Preservatives: Benzoic acid (E210)

Preservatives

Preservatives are chemicals that make food last. Natural ones like sugar, vinegar and salt, have been used for centuries.

Look at labels on cans to see what other chemicals are used as preservatives today.

Pasteurized milk is heated enough to kill dangerous microbes. It lasts a few days.

Before pasteurization, cows were led around towns and milked on the doorstep.

Food you store loses some nutrients, particularly vitamins, so it is better to eat fresh food.

Food from far away

These days food can be kept fresh for so long that shops have exotic fruits from all over the world. They travel in specially refrigerated ships.

Next time you go to a supermarket, see if it says where the fruit comes from on the shelves.

Pineapple

Mangoes

Banana Passion fruit

Lychees

What makes you hungry?

When your body needs food, it sends a message to your brain to say so. Then you look around to find something to eat.

Sometimes, when you see or smell food you like, it can make you feel hungry even though your body doesn't need food.

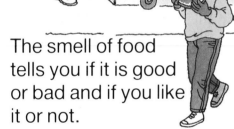

Nose smells food

Eyes see food

The smell of food tells you if it is good or bad and if you like it or not.

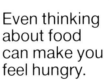

Even thinking about food can make you feel hungry.

Stomach is empty

What makes your mouth water?

When you see or smell food you like, your body gets ready to eat. You may feel water in your mouth. This is saliva, the juice your mouth makes to help mix your food.

Saliva dripping from a dog's mouth means that he is ready to eat.

Tummy rumbles

Sometimes, when your stomach is getting ready for food, it makes a rumbling noise. The sound you can hear is air and digestive juices being pushed around inside.

Tasting food

You can tell what food you do and don't like by the taste of it. Your tongue is what you mainly use to taste food. It is covered with lots of tiny bumps called taste buds.

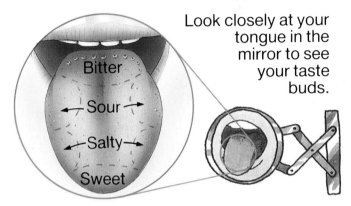

Look closely at your tongue in the mirror to see your taste buds.

Bitter
← Sour →
← Salty →
Sweet

There are four types of taste buds. Each tells a different kind of taste: salty, sweet, sour and bitter. They are on different parts of your tongue.

The smell of things helps you taste them as well. Try holding your nose when you eat. Can you taste your food?

Try this

Dip your finger in some salt. Put it on the tip of your tongue, then on the back and finally on the side. Which part can you taste it on most?

Do the same with sugar, lemon juice and coffee. Can you tell which kind of taste they are?

See if you can fill in a chart like the one below.

Food	Part of tongue	Taste
Salt		
Sugar		sweet
Lemon	Back of side	
Coffee		

Professional tasters

Some people can tell different tastes more easily than others. They may become professional wine- or tea-tasters.

Food that's bad for you

If you only ate your favourite food, your body wouldn't get all the good things it needs.

Some foods have very little goodness and can be bad for you if you eat too much of them.

Sweet things

Sugar is what makes things sweet. It is a carbohydrate so it gives you energy, but too much of it makes you fat. It also makes your teeth rot.

The more sweet things you eat, the more fillings you are likely to have at the dentist's.

Fatty food

Food that is fried, such as a burger, has lots of extra fat. It makes you feel full so you may not eat other things that are good for you.

Having extra fat is like carrying heavy bags. Your body and heart have to work harder to carry the weight.

What is junk food?

Food that has mostly bad things and very few good things in it is called junk food.

Sweets and fizzy drinks are nearly all sugar.

Ice creams, milk shakes and biscuits are mostly fat and sugar.

Fast food is often fried and so has extra fat.

40

What is a food allergy?

Some people feel bad every time they eat a certain kind of food. They may get a headache or a rash or be sick. This is called a food allergy.

One person's favourite food can make another person feel really ill.

Quite a lot of people are allergic to fish, eggs, strawberries or shellfish.

Special problems with food

Some people's bodies can't store sugar so they can only eat a little of it. Some need injections to help their body use sugar properly. This problem is called diabetes.

Some chocolate is made without sugar so that people with diabetes can enjoy it, too.

Other people's bodies don't like gluten – a protein in wheat. They can't eat things with wheat or wheat flour in them. This problem is called coeliac disease.

Can you guess which things in this picture have wheat in them? The answer is at the bottom of page 42.

Religion

Some people don't eat certain kinds of food because their religion says they shouldn't. Muslims and Jews don't eat pork, for example.

Where does food come from?

Almost everything you eat comes from a living thing: either a plant or an animal.

Plants make their own food, using energy from the sun. Animals eat plants or other animals. So do people. The way one thing eats another is called a food chain.

Energy from the sun.

You get energy from cow's milk.

Energy goes from the grass to the cow.

Bread and cereals come from corn.

Beef, cheese and milk come from cows.

In this picture, do you know where all the picnic food comes from? Can you find out what the food chain of the egg is? Turn to the bottom of page 44 for the answer.

Answer from page 41: All of them.

People who don't eat meat

People who choose not to eat any meat are called vegetarians. Some don't like the taste of meat. Others don't like to kill animals and think the way they are kept is cruel.

Some people don't eat anything at all that comes from animals. They are called vegans.

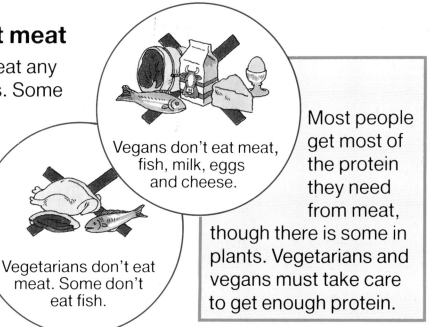

Vegans don't eat meat, fish, milk, eggs and cheese.

Vegetarians don't eat meat. Some don't eat fish.

Most people get most of the protein they need from meat, though there is some in plants. Vegetarians and vegans must take care to get enough protein.

How are animals kept?

For most farmers it is more important to produce lots of food cheaply, than it is to give an animal a nice life. This is because people usually buy cheaper food.

For example, hens usually stop laying eggs at night. But if they are kept in warm cages with the lights on, they lay for longer.

Hens that run around the farm are called free-range hens.

Hens kept in cages are called battery hens. They can lay about 270 eggs a year.

A free-range hen may only lay 80 eggs a year, so its eggs are more expensive.

Is there enough food?

If all the food in the world was spread evenly among all the people, everyone would have enough to eat. But it isn't like that.

In rich parts of the world like Europe, North America and Australia, most people get plenty to eat. Some eat too much.

Families in rich countries tend to be smaller so there are fewer people to share the food.

In poor parts of the world like Africa, Southeast Asia and South America people have a lot less to eat. Many don't get enough.

Families in these countries tend to be larger so there are more mouths to feed.

Other problems in poor countries

Without rain you cannot grow things. Some African countries have had no rain for several years and their farmland is now desert.

If there is a war, land for growing food may be destroyed. Often food from other countries can't get through to help feed people.

44   Answer from page 42: egg - chicken - corn.

What is malnutrition?

Malnutrition is when people don't get enough of the right nutrients. This means they catch diseases more easily.

In many poor countries people don't get enough protein. Children especially need protein to grow. Most protein comes from animals. They are expensive to keep so many people can't afford them.

What is a famine?

A famine is when there is so little food that people die. Often they die of diseases caused by malnutrition.

Who helps?

There are organizations in rich countries which send some food and help to places where there is famine.

Future food

If the population of the whole world keeps growing there won't be enough food for everyone, particularly meat, fish and eggs.

So scientists are busy searching for new kinds of food, especially plants with lots of protein.

Soya is a plant from China which has lots of protein. It can be made to look and taste like other food.

Some seaweeds are rich in protein. It grows all over the world but it is only eaten in a few countries, such as Japan, so far.

Around the world

People in different countries eat different things. This is because each part of the world has different plants and animals. This map shows you three main crops that grow in different parts of the world.

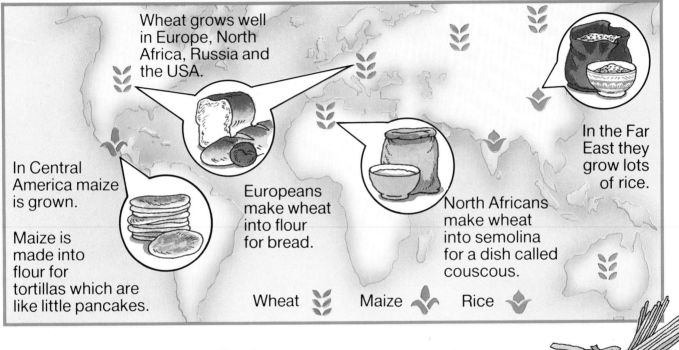

Wheat grows well in Europe, North Africa, Russia and the USA.

In Central America maize is grown.

Maize is made into flour for tortillas which are like little pancakes.

Europeans make wheat into flour for bread.

North Africans make wheat into semolina for a dish called couscous.

In the Far East they grow lots of rice.

Wheat   Maize   Rice

Food that has travelled

Lots of the food we eat every day was first found in distant countries by explorers.

Potatoes were discovered by the Spanish in South America in the 16th century.

Turkeys were also found by the Spanish, in Mexico.

Spices like cloves, pepper and cinnamon were carried back from the East in the Middle Ages.

Pasta was found in the Far East by the famous Italian explorer Marco Polo.

Unusual food

People in other countries eat all sorts of things that you may never have tried.

In some parts of the world people eat insects which have lots of protein in them.

On Chinese stalls like this one you can buy beetles, bats, snakes or even so-called 100-year-old eggs.

Insects are common food in many parts of Africa.

Ants are eaten in Columbia.

Grasshoppers are cooked and eaten in Mexico.

Ways to eat

In Western countries most people eat with a knife and fork.

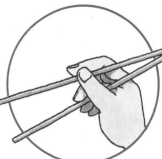

In countries in the Far East people use two wooden sticks called chopsticks.

In the Middle East people often eat together from the same dish with one hand only, always the right hand.

Holidays abroad

If you go on holiday abroad, see if you notice any different things people eat and the way they eat them.

A meal to make

Here's a whole meal you can make, which has all the good things you need. Do you know which dish has most protein? Which has lots of vitamin C? Which one is best for your teeth and bones?

Ham salad roll

You need:
- a slice of ham
- some soft cheese
- a stick of celery

Spread the cheese onto the ham.

Lay the celery at one end. Roll the ham around it.

Serve it with some brown bread.

You could put lettuce inside too.

Yogurt drink

You need:
- a glass of milk
- a pot of fruit yogurt

Put the yogurt in a jug. Add the milk and whisk until frothy.

You could add another fruit.

Banana kebabs

You need:
- a banana • lemon juice • dessicated coconut • a skewer

Peel and cut the banana into rounds.

Soak the rounds in lemon juice.

Dip each round in coconut and thread on the skewer.

Answers: The ham roll has most protein. The banana kebab has most vitamin C. The yogurt drink is best for your teeth and bones because it has calcium and vitamin D.

48

What Makes You Ill?

Contents

All about being ill

Most of the time you probably feel well. Your body can do lots of things without you even thinking about them.

Your brain lets you think clearly.

Most of the time you are happy and feel comfortable inside.

Your skin looks smooth and healthy.

You feel energetic and want to run around and play.

Your arms and legs feel strong.

You get hungry if you have not eaten for a while.

Ill or well?

You can usually tell if you are ill because things feel wrong with your body. These things are called symptoms. You can often tell what is wrong by the kind of symptoms you have.

You may feel hot one minute, then cold the next.

Your tummy may feel shaky and you may need to be sick.

You feel miserable, and do not want to join in your friends' games.

You might feel tired and achy and want to lie down.

You might have a pain somewhere.

You may lose your appetite.

What is pain?

Having a pain is one way your body tells you something is wrong.

Sometimes you can easily see what is wrong because of where it hurts.

Sometimes you have a pain in one place when really the problem is somewhere else. Tonsillitis causes a tummy ache, even though your tonsils are in your throat.

Getting better

Your body is good at getting better by itself. You can help it mend by resting. There are lots of ways to keep busy while you rest.

Watching TV

Reading

Playing games

Listening to music

Plenty of love and attention from your family or friends can make you feel better too.

If resting doesn't help, and you don't get better on your own, you may have to visit your doctor.

Keeping well

Looking after yourself helps you stay well. Eating the right food and exercising keep you fit. Being fit helps you fight illness and get better more quickly if you are ill.

Sports and energetic games keep you fit.

Fruit is a healthy food to eat.

Why do you get ill?

People become ill for many different reasons. Most everyday illnesses are caused by germs. Your body usually fights germs off but sometimes they make you ill. This is called having an infection.

There are many different kinds of germ. They cause different symptoms of infection.

Sore throat

Headache

Tummy ache

Rash

Sneezing sprays millions of germs into the air.

Most germs are spread through the air. When you have a cold you breathe out germs all the time. If people around you breathe them in they may catch your cold.

Where you live

Where you live can affect your health. For example, traffic fumes and factory smoke can pollute the air you breathe. This can make people ill.

Accidents

Sometimes accidents can hurt you or make you ill. Many accidents happen at home.

Falling can give you cuts or bruises or even break your bones.

Hot things can burn you. Always be careful with hot food.

Feelings

Your feelings can make you ill too. Worrying may upset your tummy and make you feel sick.

Feeling nervous about your first day at a new school can make you feel ill.

Family illnesses

Some illnesses tend to run in families. Scientists now know someone is more likely to get asthma if one of their parents has it. Asthma makes it difficult to breathe properly.

People with asthma can take medicine to help them run around and play sports.

Allergies

Ordinary things like cat hair, pollen from plants, and certain foods make some people feel poorly. This is called having an allergy.

An allergy to strawberries can give you a rash.

53

What is a germ?

Germs are tiny, living things. They are everywhere: in the air you breathe, on your skin, in your food and on the things you touch.

The three main kinds of germs are called bacteria, viruses and fungi.

Germs are so tiny you need a microscope to see them.

There are germs inside your body all the time. Most of them don't do you any harm. Some can even be helpful, but others make you ill.

Some useful bacteria live in your tummy. They help you to digest your food.

Bacteria

Bacteria are so tiny that over a thousand could fit on a pinhead. Some can cause illnesses such as ear and skin infections.

These bacteria cause earache. They are magnified many times so you can see them.

Viruses

Viruses are over a million times smaller than bacteria. They cause many common infections such as colds, tummy upsets and sore throats.

This kind of virus causes sore throats.

If you look at viruses through very strong microscopes, you can see their strange shapes.

Keeping germs out

Your body is built to keep harmful germs out as much as possible. This picture shows how your body protects you.

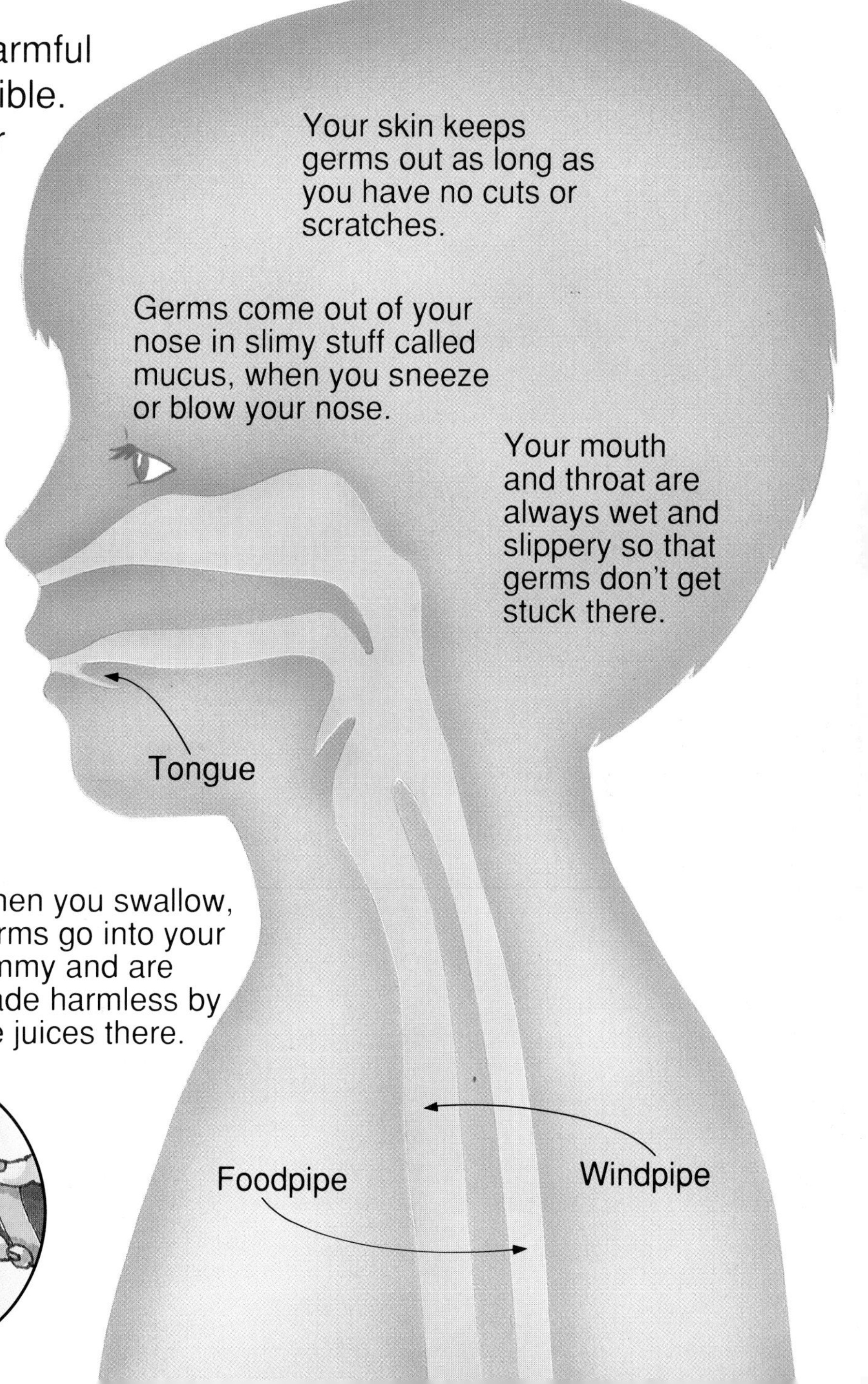

Eyelashes stop dirt and germs from getting into your eyes.

You have tears in your eyes all the time. They help wash out germs.

Tiny hairs in your nose catch germs you breathe in.

Your skin keeps germs out as long as you have no cuts or scratches.

Germs come out of your nose in slimy stuff called mucus, when you sneeze or blow your nose.

Your mouth and throat are always wet and slippery so that germs don't get stuck there.

Tongue

When you swallow, germs go into your tummy and are made harmless by the juices there.

Foodpipe

Windpipe

Fungi

These are germs which grow on your body and cause infections. Athlete's foot is a fungus which can grow between your toes. It makes your skin look sore and flaky.

You can get rid of athlete's foot with special powder.

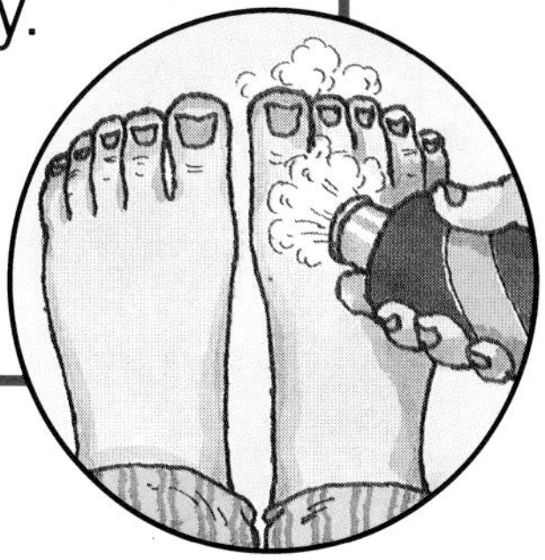

Germ attack

Your whole body is made up of millions of tiny living parts called cells. When germs such as bacteria or viruses get into your body they start to multiply and feed off your cells. This makes you feel ill.

Bacteria invasion

Your body is a warm, damp place with plenty of food, so bacteria grow and spread quickly inside you. Within hours there can be millions in one small part of your body.

This is what cells from your skin look like through a very strong microscope.

Some bacteria attack your cells by giving off poisons. These can also spread infection around your body in your blood.

Cell

Poisons

Bacteria

Bacteria attack cell with poisons.

Virus invasion

Viruses attack by getting inside a cell. The cell becomes a kind of factory for making new viruses.

Virus enters cell.

New viruses are made inside cell.

Cells die and viruses set out to invade new cells.

Germs and symptoms

Symptoms are caused both by germs damaging your cells, and by the way your body fights back. Different germs cause symptoms in different parts of your body.

An area infected by bacteria, such as an aching tooth, often feels sore and swollen.

Your temperature rises as your body starts to fight the germs. This is an early sign of infection.

Colds and flu often start with a sore throat because the viruses that cause them start in your throat.

Cleaning cuts and protecting them with a plaster or bandage helps to stop bacteria from getting in.

A medicine called paracetamol helps lower your temperature.

In the blood

Your blood is always flowing inside you. It takes food and oxygen around your body. But it can also help spread any infections that get into your blood.

Getting better

Medicines called antibiotics can help treat illnesses caused by bacteria. No medicines can get rid of viruses. Your body fights them in its own way.

Fighting back

When you get an infection your body fights off the invading germs. In your blood there are special cells to try and stop them from spreading further.

The germ eaters

When germs damage your cells, more blood flows to the infected place. White blood cells then devour the germs.

Germ

1. White blood cell sticks to germs.

2. White blood cell surrounds germs.

3. Germs are digested inside.

In your blood

This page shows a close-up picture of blood vessels. These are the tubes that carry blood around your body. Blood contains millions of cells in a liquid called plasma. Red blood cells carry food and oxygen. White blood cells have the job of killing germs.

Plasma

White blood cell

Red blood cell

Flushing out germs

Lymph is a liquid that runs around your body in a network of tubes. It carries dead germs and cells to swellings called lymph nodes. Here, white blood cells clean them out of the lymph.

Lymph nodes

Lymph tubes

Lymph nodes, especially in your neck, can feel sore and swollen while you are fighting germs.

Permanent protection

During an infection, special white blood cells called lymphocytes kill germs using chemicals known as antibodies.

Antibody

1. Antibodies hold onto germ.

2. Germ bursts open and dies.

Germ

Antibodies can recognize germs that have attacked you before. They stay in your body to stop the same germs from attacking again. This means you only catch most infections once. Being protected like this is called being immune.

Immunization

Immunization is a way of making you immune to an infectious illness without your ever having to catch it.

When you are immunized, you are given a tiny dose of a germ. The dose is too weak to make you ill, but it helps your body produce the antibodies that will protect you against that illness in the future.

Babies are usually given injections that immunize them against some serious illnesses.

59

Allergies

An allergy is when your body fights ordinary things as if they were germs. This can cause symptoms such as a rash, wheezing or tummy ache. Anything that causes an allergy in somebody is called an allergen.

What happens

When an allergen invades the body of an allergic person, white blood cells send out antibodies to fight it. A chemical called histamine is produced, which causes the allergic symptoms.

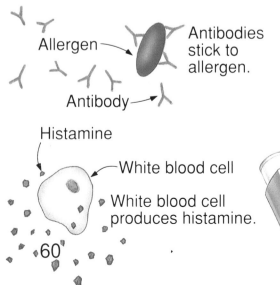

Allergen

Antibody

Antibodies stick to allergen.

Histamine

White blood cell

White blood cell produces histamine.

Breathing

Some people are allergic to things they breathe in, such as dust, pollen, feathers or pet hairs.

Hay fever can be caused by an allergy to pollen. It makes you sneeze and your eyes become watery and itchy.

What is asthma?

Asthma can be caused by an allergy. It makes it difficult to breathe air into your lungs, so you wheeze or cough. Here you can see what happens.

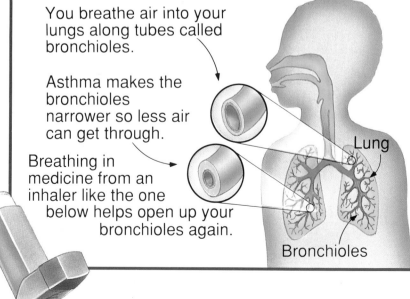

You breathe air into your lungs along tubes called bronchioles.

Asthma makes the bronchioles narrower so less air can get through.

Breathing in medicine from an inhaler like the one below helps open up your bronchioles again.

Lung

Bronchioles

Touching

Some people have to be careful what they wear against their skin. Metal, for instance in earrings, and material such as wool, can cause a rash.

An itchy rash called eczema is sometimes caused by washing powder or soap.

Metal

Wool

WASHO

Eating

Some people are allergic to certain foods. Eating them can cause allergic symptoms including a tummy ache or rash. Food allergy can play a part in asthma.

These foods can cause allergies in some people.

Milk

Seafood

Chocolate

Treating allergies

You cannot catch allergies from other people. The best protection against them is for people to try to avoid things they know they are allergic to.

It is hard to avoid allergens such as dust which get everywhere. People allergic to dust need their bedrooms cleaned or dusted regularly.

Medicines called antihistamines can ease some of the symptoms caused by allergies.

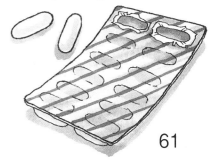

61

How illnesses spread

The most common way that illnesses are spread is through the air. When you

cough, sneeze or breathe out, you spray tiny droplets into the air. This can spread illnesses such as colds, flu and chickenpox to other people.

Covering your mouth and nose when you cough or sneeze helps stop germs from spreading. One sneeze can shoot germs over three metres (10 feet).

Touching

Some skin infections, such as cold sores or warts, can be spread from one person to another by touching the infected place.

Try not to share other people's things, such as towels or unwashed dishes and cutlery, if they have an infection.

Food

If you do not take enough care with food, germs can make it bad and cause illness.
Bacteria grow on fresh food such as meat and milk if it is kept for too long.

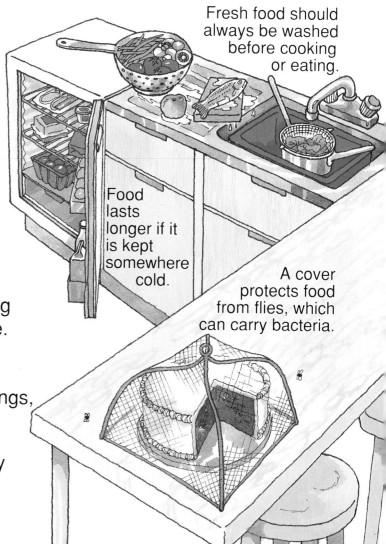

Fresh food should always be washed before cooking or eating.

Food lasts longer if it is kept somewhere cold.

A cover protects food from flies, which can carry bacteria.

Washing hands

Always wash your hands after going to the toilet, and before eating or handling food. Dirty hands can spread germs onto food and cause bad upset tummies.

Soil can occasionally carry a serious disease caused by dog or cat mess, so take care to wash your hands after playing outside in parks or gardens.

Occasionally some pets can pass on diseases. It is always best to wash your hands after handling animals, and not to kiss them, or let them lick your face.

Headlice

Headlice are tiny creatures that can live in your hair and make your head feel itchy. Lice and their eggs (called nits) can get from one person's head to another's.

Tie long hair back for school, and don't share brushes or combs.

Bad water

Water can also carry diseases. This sometimes happens in poorer places where people have to share the same dirty water for washing, drinking and cooking.

Infected water can spread diseases to many people.

63

Accidents

If ever you get hurt or injured, whether it is a tiny cut or a broken leg, your body has its own ways of mending itself.

Cuts and grazes

If your skin is broken by a cut or graze and your blood vessels are damaged, blood flows out of your body. Tiny blood cells called platelets soon stop the bleeding by making a sticky plug called a clot.

Bumps and bruises

A hard bump can damage blood vessels without breaking your skin. Blood leaks out underneath your skin, but it cannot escape. This causes a bruise.

Chemicals from red blood cells can make bruises look purple.

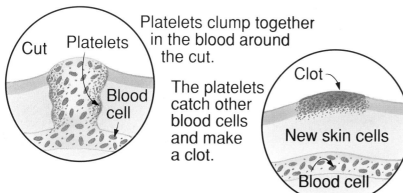

Cut Platelets

Platelets clump together in the blood around the cut.

Blood cell

The platelets catch other blood cells and make a clot.

Clot

New skin cells

Blood cell

A bump on a bony part of your body, such as your shin or head, can cause a lump. Your skin swells because there is less room underneath for the blood to drain away.

A blood clot becomes a scab which protects the cut while it heals. Underneath, new skin cells are made to replace the damaged ones. Soon the scab dries up and falls off.

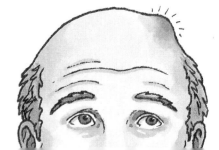

64

Broken bones

If a bone gets broken, your body has to make new cells to grow over the break and join the bone together again. The bone must be set (put) in the right position and kept still while it mends.

Special photographs called X-rays show where and how the bone is broken.

Break

Plaster cast keeps leg still.

Burns

When a burn damages your skin, watery fluid wells up from underneath and forms a blister.

Burned skin

Fluid

Cold water can ease the pain of a burn and help stop the damage from spreading.

Blisters help protect damaged cells. When new cells grow underneath, the fluid disappears and the old, damaged skin peels away.

65

Going to the doctor

Sometimes you may need help from a doctor to get better. A doctor's job is to recognize an illness and try to put things right.

Finding out what's wrong

The doctor asks you questions about how you are feeling. If you can describe your symptoms clearly, it helps her to tell what is wrong. She also looks and feels for any signs of illness such as a rash or swelling.

The doctor may feel your neck. If the lymph nodes there are swollen, it shows you have an infection.

She may put a thermometer under your tongue to take your temperature. It should be about 37°C (98.4°F).

A stethoscope makes sounds inside you louder so she can check that your heart and lungs are working properly.

Records of your health and past visits give the doctor clues to what is wrong.

She uses a special light to look inside your ears, throat and eyes.

When a doctor is working out what is wrong with you, it is called making a diagnosis. Once she has done this, the doctor can then give you advice about getting better.

Hospital

Occasionally your doctor may decide to send you to a hospital. Here you can see another doctor who knows all about your particular illness. In different parts of a hospital doctors treat different illnesses.

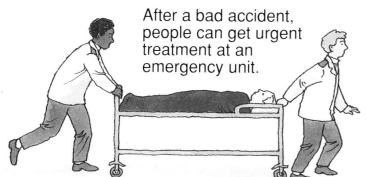

After a bad accident, people can get urgent treatment at an emergency unit.

If you have to stay in a hospital for a while, nurses will look after you. A close member of your family may be able to stay with you and friends can visit to cheer you up.

Medicine

Sometimes doctors have to prescribe medicine to help you get better. Medicines must be used just as the doctor says, otherwise they may not work, or could be dangerous.

2 spoonfuls twice a day.

Doctors on the move

In parts of the world far from towns, people cannot easily get to a doctor so doctors travel to see them. They stay a short while in each place to give people treatment, and advice about staying healthy.

Where you live

People's health is affected by where they live, what they do and how much money they have. Different illnesses are found in different parts of the world.

Weather

The weather can affect people's health. For instance, in hot, wet parts of the world, mosquitoes can spread a serious disease called malaria.

Mosquitoes can infect people with malaria when they bite them.

Food

In some poorer parts of the world, there is not always enough food to go around. Without all the goodness they need from food, people can get very ill. This is called malnutrition.

Red areas on this map show poorer parts of the world.

AFRICA

In parts of Africa, many people die every year from malnutrition.

Not all food is good for you. In richer parts of the world many people suffer from diseases which doctors think may be caused by eating too much of the wrong kind of food.

This meal has lots of sugar and fat, which is bad for you.

68

Pollution

Pollution can harm all living things, including people. For instance, polluted lakes and rivers can make people ill if the water gets into their drinking supplies.

Overcrowding

Illness can spread quickly in places where people live crowded together without good health care. A disease that infects many people at one time in this way is called an epidemic.

In 1990 an epidemic of cholera in South America affected many people who lived in poor places like the one in this picture.

Jobs

The places where people work, and the jobs they do, can affect their health.

People who work down mines can suffer breathing problems from the dust.

Knowing the facts

Learning about how your body works and how illnesses happen helps you live a healthier life.

Years ago nobody knew that smoking caused serious heart and lung diseases. Now people can learn to stay healthier by not smoking.

69

Staying healthy

There are lots of things you can do to help you stay healthy. These are some of them.

Eating well

You need to eat many different types of food to stay really healthy. How much you eat is important too. Eating too much or too little can be unhealthy.

Foods like rice, pasta and potatoes give you energy.

Meat, chicken and fish help you grow.

Dairy products such as cheese make your bones and teeth grow strong.

Keeping yourself clean

Keeping your body clean can help stop germs from causing infections.

Washing and brushing your hair helps keep headlice away.

Brushing your teeth regularly helps prevent tooth decay. Tiny pieces of food that stick in your mouth can produce acids which rot your teeth.

Cleaning your fingernails gets rid of any dirt that might carry germs.

Cuts and grazes should be washed and kept protected.

Washing your hands after going to the toilet or before eating helps stop many germs from spreading.

Fruit and vegetables contain vitamins which keep your body working well.

PASTA

Being careful

You can avoid many accidents and injuries by being careful of things that can harm you.

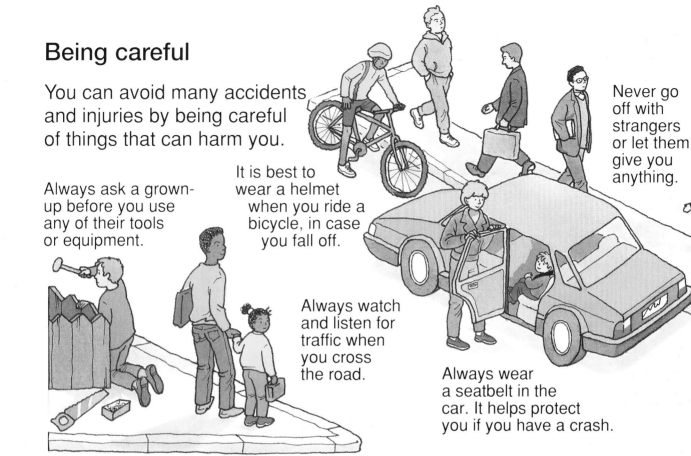

Always ask a grown-up before you use any of their tools or equipment.

It is best to wear a helmet when you ride a bicycle, in case you fall off.

Always watch and listen for traffic when you cross the road.

Never go off with strangers or let them give you anything.

Always wear a seatbelt in the car. It helps protect you if you have a crash.

Exercise

Exercising is a good way of looking after your body. It keeps it in good working order and helps prevent illness.

Swimming is good for people with asthma because it helps improve their breathing.

Feeling good

If ever you feel worried or upset, it can help to talk to somebody you know well and trust. Your friends and family can often make you feel better. Having friends and feeling loved is good for everybody's health.

Health quiz

Here are some questions to see how much you can remember from this part of the book. If you get stuck, look back at the pages for help. Write your answers down, then check them at the bottom of this page.

1. When you are well, what should your body temperature be?

(a) about 35°C (95.0°F)
(b) about 36°C (96.8°F)
(c) about 37°C (98.4°F)

2. Which of these has the job of killing germs in your body?

(a) red blood cells
(b) white blood cells
(c) platelets

3. One of these things protects a cut while it heals. Which is it?

(a) a bruise
(b) a blister
(c) a scab

4. All of these are kinds of germs, except for one. Which one does not belong?

(a) bacteria
(b) plasma
(c) fungus
(d) virus

5. Which of these things can make people ill?

(a) pollution
(b) eating unhealthy food
(c) insects
(d) not enough food

6. Which of these is not part of your body?

(a) bronchioles
(b) an epidemic
(c) a lymph node

Answers: 1(c) 2(b) 3(c) 4(b) Plasma is the liquid part of your blood. 5 All of them. 6(b) An epidemic is a disease which infects lots of people at once.

Where Do Babies Come From?

Contents

All about babies

As the baby grows, its mother's tummy gets bigger.

Everybody who has ever lived was once a baby and grew in their mother's tummy. This part of the book tells the story of how babies come into the world and begin to grow up.

A baby grows in a sort of hollow bag called the womb or uterus. This is a warm, safe place for it to be until it is big and strong enough to survive in the outside world.

Food and oxygen

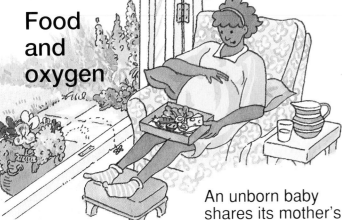

An unborn baby shares its mother's food and oxygen.

Being born

The baby needs food to stay alive and grow. It also needs oxygen from the air. But babies cannot eat or breathe in the womb. They get food and oxygen from their mother's blood.

The baby stays inside its mother for about nine months. That is about 38 weeks. Then it is ready to be born. It gets out of its mother's tummy through an opening between her legs.

74

Feeding

At first the only food a baby needs is milk, either from her mother's breasts or from feeding bottles. She needs to be fed every few hours.

Crying

It is not always easy to work out what a baby's crying means.

A newborn baby can do nothing for herself so she takes a lot of looking after. Crying is her only way of telling people she needs something.

Baby animals

A cow's tummy gets fatter as her calf grows inside her.

Kittens feed on milk from their mother's nipples.

Many animals grow in their mothers' tummies and are born in the same way as people. They also get milk from their mothers.

Growing up

Babies gradually learn to do more and more for themselves.

Many animals separate from their parents when they are very young. It is years before children can manage without their parents' help.

Starting to grow

Everybody is made of millions of tiny living bits called cells. A baby starts to grow from just two very special cells, one from its mother and one from its father. Together, these two cells make one new cell.

Dividing cells

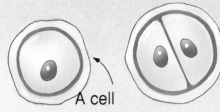

A cell

The new cell divides in half to make two cells exactly the same. These two cells then divide to make four cells. The cells carry on dividing until a whole ball of cells is made.

Each cell is really no bigger than one of the full stops on this page.

In the womb

Ball of cells

Womb lining

Womb

The ball of cells settles down in the mother's womb, the place where babies grow. It sinks into the womb's soft cushiony lining and carries on growing.

A month later, the developing baby is still no bigger than a baked bean; but the dividing cells have started growing into the different parts of the baby's body.

Brain

Backbone

Eye

The baby's heart is already beating.

Arm

Leg

The baby's lifeline

The baby is attached to the lining of the womb by a special cord. The food and oxygen the baby needs go from its mother's blood down the cord and into the baby's body.

Like everybody else, the baby needs to get rid of waste. This goes down the cord from the baby's blood into its mother's blood. Her body gets rid of it when she goes to the toilet.

Blood vessels

This is called the placenta. It grows on the lining of the womb.

The cord is called the umbilical cord.

The placenta is where food and oxygen, and waste, pass between the mother's blood and the baby's.

The baby floats in a bag of special water. This cushions it from knocks.

The baby cannot drown in the water because it does not need to breathe until it is born.

Getting bigger

The baby continues to grow. It moves and kicks, and also sleeps. It can hear its mother's heart beating and noises from outside her body too. Some babies even get hiccups.

Eventually, most babies settle into an upside-down position in the womb.

Some babies suck their thumbs.

77

What is it like being pregnant?

When a mother has a baby growing inside her, it is called being pregnant. While she is pregnant, her body changes in all sorts of ways.

Check-ups

The mother has regular check-ups to make sure she and the baby are healthy. These are given by a midwife or doctor. A midwife is someone who looks after pregnant mothers.

The mother is weighed. She should put on weight as the baby grows.

The mother's blood and urine (wee) are tested. This helps the midwife tell if the mother and baby are well.

Looking after herself

The mother has to take special care of herself. If she is well, the baby is more likely to be healthy too.

It is not good for the baby if the mother smokes, drinks alcohol or takes certain medicines.

She is feeding her baby as well as herself, so she has to eat healthy food.

The mother's body has to work harder than usual, giving the baby what it needs. She has to rest more.

Gentle exercise pumps more blood through to the baby and makes the mother feel better too.

When the mother's tummy gets big, she should not carry heavy things. She may strain her back.

The midwife feels the mother's tummy. This gives her an idea of the baby's size and position.

She listens to the baby's heart through a special stethoscope. She puts it on the mother's tummy.

Photos of the baby

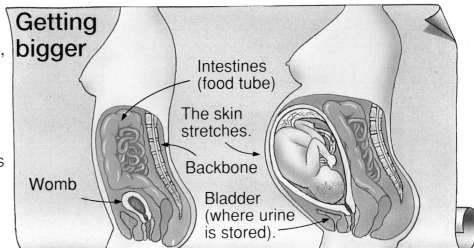

Head
Arm
Body
Leg

A machine called an ultrasound scanner takes moving pictures of the baby in the womb. These appear on a television screen and show everyone how the baby is developing.

Kicking

After about five months, the mother feels the baby moving. Later, it will kick.

You may feel the kicks if you put your hand on the mother's tummy.

Eventually the mother can see her tummy moving and even guess whether a bump is a hand or a foot.

Getting bigger

Intestines (food tube)
The skin stretches.
Backbone
Womb
Bladder (where urine is stored).

The mother's womb is normally the size of a small pear. As the baby grows, the womb stretches and other things in her body get squashed up. This can be a bit uncomfortable but everything goes back to normal later.

Mothers and fathers

The special cells from the mother and father which make a baby start to grow are the sex cells. They are different from each other.

Egg cells

The mother's sex cell is called an egg cell or ovum. She has lots of egg cells stored in her body, near her womb.

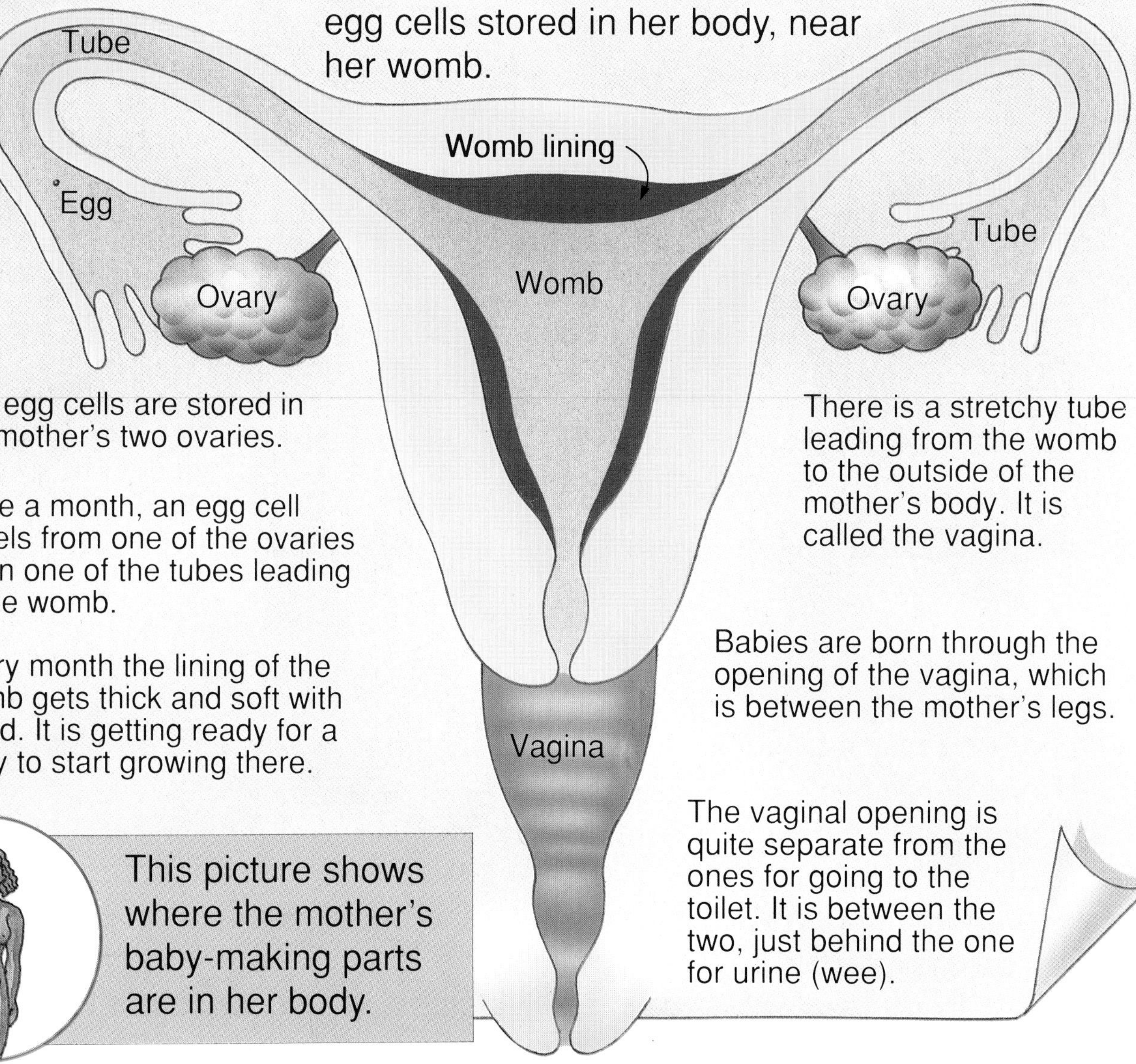

Tube

Womb lining

Egg

Tube

Ovary

Womb

Ovary

The egg cells are stored in the mother's two ovaries.

Once a month, an egg cell travels from one of the ovaries down one of the tubes leading to the womb.

Every month the lining of the womb gets thick and soft with blood. It is getting ready for a baby to start growing there.

There is a stretchy tube leading from the womb to the outside of the mother's body. It is called the vagina.

Babies are born through the opening of the vagina, which is between the mother's legs.

Vagina

The vaginal opening is quite separate from the ones for going to the toilet. It is between the two, just behind the one for urine (wee).

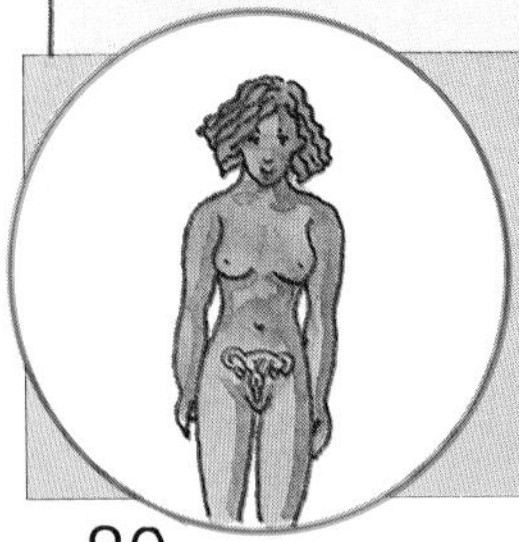

This picture shows where the mother's baby-making parts are in her body.

Sperm

The father's sex cell is called a sperm cell. Sperm are made in the father's two testicles. The testicles are in the bag of skin which hangs behind his penis (willy).

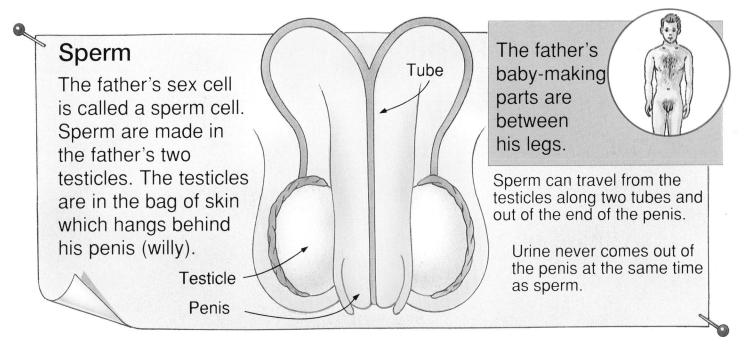

Tube

Testicle

Penis

The father's baby-making parts are between his legs.

Sperm can travel from the testicles along two tubes and out of the end of the penis.

Urine never comes out of the penis at the same time as sperm.

Growing up

Young girls and boys cannot become mothers and fathers. Your baby-making parts do not start working properly until the time when your body starts to look like a grown-up's.

What if a baby doesn't start?

If a baby does not start to grow, the womb's thick lining is not needed. The lining and the egg cell break up and trickle out of the mother's vagina with some blood.

This takes a few days each month and is called having a period. To soak up what comes out, the mother puts things called tampons in her vagina or pads in her pants.

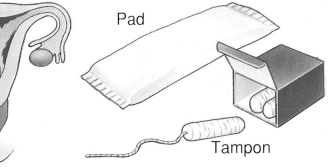

Pad

Tampon

How does a baby start?

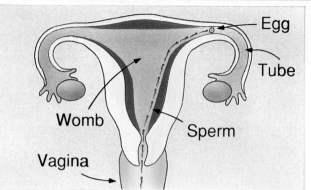

A baby starts to grow when an egg and sperm meet and join together. They do this inside the mother's body. The way the sperm get to the egg is through the mother's vagina.

Sperm cells come out of the opening at the end of the penis and swim up into the mother's womb and tubes. If the sperm meet an egg in the tubes, one of them may join with it.

The mother and father cuddle each other very close. The father's penis gets stiffer and fits comfortably inside the mother's vagina. This is called making love or having sex.

Sperm have long tails which they flick. This helps them to swim.

The moment when the egg and sperm join together is called conception or fertilization. Now a baby can start to grow.

82

Sperm are so small that you can really only see them through a microscope.

Egg cells are the biggest cells in the human body. Even so, they can only just be seen without a microscope.

One sperm breaks into the egg. It leaves its tail behind.

The rest of the sperm will die.

Pregnant or not?

It is several months before the mother's tummy starts to get

Calendar

If she is pregnant, her monthly periods stop. The lining of the womb is needed for the growing baby.

The hormones may make the mother go off foods she usually likes; or they may make her crave some foods.

bigger but she has other ways of knowing she is pregnant.

Some pregnant mothers feel sick. This is caused by chemicals called hormones in their blood.

Her breasts get bigger and may feel a bit sore. They are getting ready to make milk when the baby is born.

To be sure she is pregnant, the mother's urine is tested to see if it has one of the pregnancy hormones in it.

How is a baby born?

After nine months inside its mother, the baby is ready to be born. It has to leave the warm, safe womb and move down the vagina to the outside world. This is called labour, which means hard work.

Labour

The womb is really a very strong muscle. During labour, it keeps on squeezing and squeezing until the baby comes out of it. Each squeeze is called a contraction.

The baby will not need its placenta for much longer.

The mother's other leg has been left out of this picture so you can see the baby clearly.

Vagina

The contractions pull the womb open and squeeze the baby through the opening.

Placenta

The vagina stretches easily to let the baby pass through. Afterwards it goes back to its normal size.

During labour, the bag of water around the baby bursts. The water drains away out of the mother's vagina.

Towards the end of labour, the mother pushes hard to help the baby out. Soon after the baby is born, the placenta and empty water bag come out of the vagina too.

When does labour start?

When the baby is ready to be born, special hormones are made in its blood. These go down the umbilical cord to the mother's body and make the contractions start.

The mother feels the contractions as pains in her tummy.

Most mothers go to hospital to have their baby. Some choose to have theirs at home.

Helping the mother

Having a baby is exciting but can be exhausting and take many hours. A midwife looks after the mother during labour. The father can help too.

The mother can have an injection to relieve the pain. Breathing in a mixture of a special gas and air through a face-mask also helps.

The father might rub the mother's back if it aches, or encourage her to relax and breathe properly.

The baby's heartbeat

The midwife listens to the baby's heartbeat during labour to make sure it is all right. In hospitals, the heartbeat is sometimes measured by a machine called a monitor.

The monitor is connected up to the mother's tummy.

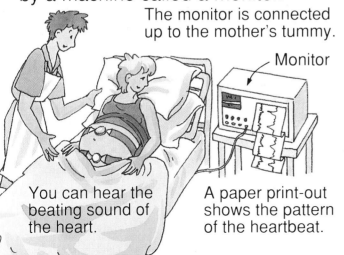

Monitor

You can hear the beating sound of the heart.

A paper print-out shows the pattern of the heartbeat.

What is a Caesarian birth?

Sometimes the baby cannot be born in the usual way. Instead it is lifted out through a cut in the mother's tummy. This is called a Caesarian.

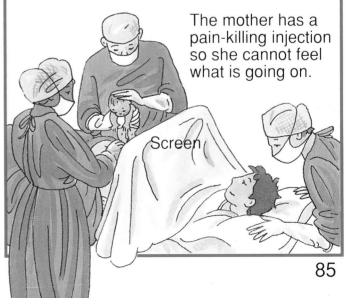

The mother has a pain-killing injection so she cannot feel what is going on.

Screen

85

Newborn babies

The first thing everyone does as soon as a baby is born is to look between its legs. Is it a girl or a boy?

The midwife checks that there is no liquid in the baby's nose or mouth. Now he can start to breathe.

The cord is cut here. The baby cannot feel it.

A clip stops any bleeding.

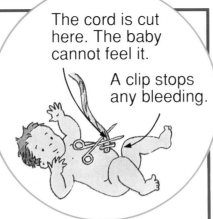

Now that the baby can breathe and feed for himself, he no longer needs his umbilical cord. It is cut off.

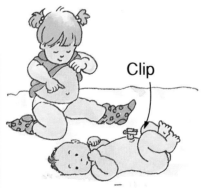

Clip

The tiny bit of cord that is left dries up and falls off in a few days. Your tummy button is where your cord was.

The midwife checks that the baby is well and weighs him. He will be weighed often to make sure he is growing.

In hospital, a newborn baby has a name label put on his wrist. This avoids any mix-up about whose baby he is.

Name label

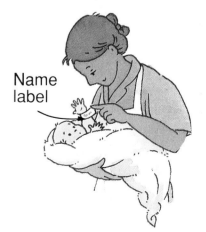

Getting used to the world

The baby has been safe and comfortable in the womb for nine months. It is probably quite a shock to find herself in the outside world. She may also be tired from the birth.

The baby will get used to her new surroundings better if she is handled and spoken to very gently. It may also help if things are kept fairly quiet and dimly lit at first.

The mother starts feeding the baby.

The parents cuddle the baby and start getting to know her. Sisters and brothers come to meet her.

Newborn babies have to be wrapped up warm. Their bodies lose heat quickly.

Some newborn babies are almost bald. Others have a lot of hair. Some have hair on their body too. This soon rubs off.

Babies have a soft patch on their head. Bones gradually grow over it but until then it has to be protected from knocks.

Babies born in hospital usually sleep in a see-through cot by their mother's bed.

At first, many babies have blue eyes. The colour may gradually change.

Incubators

If a baby is very small or unwell when she is born, she may have to go in an incubator for a while. This is a see-through cot which is all enclosed and very warm.

The parents can touch the baby through windows in the incubator.

What makes a baby like it is?

The mother's egg and the father's sperm cell together have all the instructions needed for a baby to grow in the way it does.

Chromosomes

The instructions are carried on special threads in the cells. The threads are called chromosomes. The proper word for the instructions is genes.

This picture shows part of a chromosome.

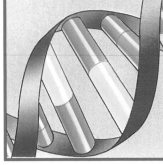

The instructions are in a complicated code a bit like a computer program.

When the egg and sperm join together at conception, the new cell gets the chromosomes from both of them. Copies of these are passed to every cell in the baby's body.

The baby's cells have 46 chromosomes each, 23 from the egg and 23 from the sperm.

Because you have chromosomes from both your parents, you will take after both of them. The mixture of the two sets of instructions also means that you are unique.

Some things about you, like the way you look, depend a lot on your chromosomes. Other things depend as well on the type of life you have after you are born.

You are more likely to become a good swimmer if you are taken to the swimming pool a lot.

Girl or boy?

Whether a baby is to be a girl or a boy is settled at conception. It depends on one chromosome in the egg and one in the sperm. These are the sex chromosomes.

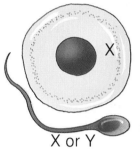

X

X or Y

The sex chromosome in all egg cells is called X. Half the sperm also have an X sex chromosome but half have one called Y.

If a sperm with an X chromosome joins with the egg, the baby is a girl.

Girls have two X sex chromosomes.

XX

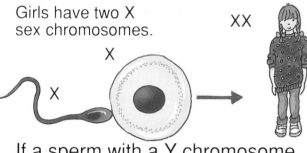

X

X

If a sperm with a Y chromosome joins with the egg, the baby is a boy.

Boys have one X and one Y sex chromosome.

XY

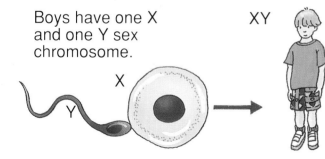

X

Y

Twins

Twins grow in their mother's womb together and are born at the same time, one by one. A few twins are identical, which means exactly alike. Most twins are non-identical, which means not exactly alike.

Sometimes, when the new cell made at conception splits in two, each half grows into a separate baby. These twins are identical because they come from the same egg and sperm.

Identical twins are always the same sex.

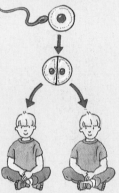

Sometimes, two separate sperm meet and join with two different eggs at the same time, and two babies grow. These twins are not identical because they come from different eggs and sperm.

Non-identical twins may be the same sex or one of each sex.

What do babies need?

Babies need to have everything done for them. They have to be fed and kept warm, comfortable and clean.

They need lots of love and attention, and they need interesting things going on around them.

Breast-feeding

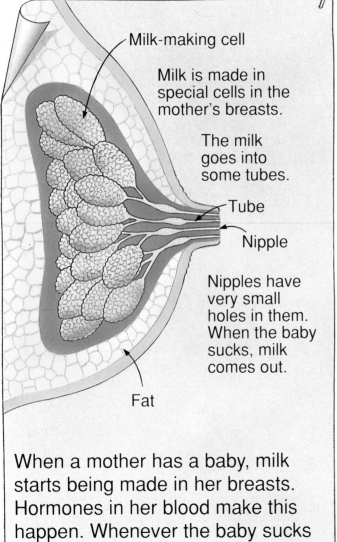

Milk-making cell

Milk is made in special cells in the mother's breasts.

The milk goes into some tubes.

Tube

Nipple

Nipples have very small holes in them. When the baby sucks, milk comes out.

Fat

When a mother has a baby, milk starts being made in her breasts. Hormones in her blood make this happen. Whenever the baby sucks at the breast, more milk is made.

If a mother is breast-feeding, she needs to eat well, drink plenty and get extra rest.

Breast milk is made from goodness in the mother's blood and is the best food for a baby. It has chemicals called antibodies in it. These help the baby to fight off illnesses.

Bottle-feeding

If babies are not being breast-fed, they have special powdered milk instead. This is usually made from cow's milk but is then altered to make it more like breast milk.

Special powdered milk is mixed with water for a baby's bottle.

Ordinary cow's milk is too strong for babies.

Cuddles

A young baby's neck is not strong enough to hold her head up. Her head needs something to rest on all the time.

A cushion will stop your arm aching.

Babies need a lot of cuddles to make them feel safe and contented. They need to be handled gently though.

Babies cannot fight off germs like older people, so their bottles have to be extra-specially clean. This is done by sterilizing, which means getting rid of germs.

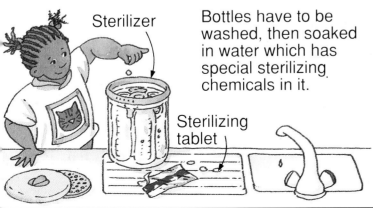

Sterilizer

Bottles have to be washed, then soaked in water which has special sterilizing chemicals in it.

Sterilizing tablet

Nappies

A young baby may need as many as eight nappy-changes in a day.

If a wet or dirty nappy is not changed, the baby is more likely to get an itchy rash.

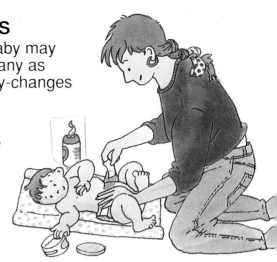

Babies do not know in advance that they need to go to the toilet. They only learn to tell as they get older.

Sleeping

Babies have no idea of day and night at first.

It can take them a long time to learn to sleep through the night.

Some young babies sleep for as many as 18 hours a day. They wake up every few hours to feed though, even in the night. Nobody knows why some babies sleep more than others.

A new baby in the family

This is an exciting, enjoyable time but it is also hard work. And it can take a while to get used to having a brand-new person in the family.

A new baby takes up so much of her parents' time and attention that older brothers and sisters can even feel a bit jealous at first.

The mother's body

It takes a few weeks for the mother's body to go back to normal after having the baby, and she needs to rest. Both parents will be tired from getting up in the night to the baby.

Helping

You could fetch things that are needed for the baby and tidy them away.

It is useful for the parents to have help around the house at first. As the baby gets older, you may be able to help by, say, giving her a bottle.

92

Crying

A baby's crying is hard to ignore. This is useful for the baby: it makes people look after him. Babies cry for various reasons. Nobody really knows why some cry more than others.

Is the baby hungry? Is he uncomfortable or in pain? Is he too hot or too cold, bored, tired, lonely or frightened?

Babies cannot wait for things. They have not learned to think about other people's feelings and if they do have to wait long, for something like food, they may even become unwell.

Brothers and sisters can sometimes feel left out.

Playing with a baby

A new baby will not be able to play with you for some time but she may soon start to enjoy watching you play nearby. Once you start to play with her, try to move and speak gently so you don't startle her. Give her plenty of time to react to things and remember that babies cannot concentrate for long. Never do anything she is not happy about.

Babies can only see clearly about 25cm (10in) from their nose.

Babies learn about things by putting them in their mouth, so always ask a grown-up if they are safe.

For the first few weeks, a baby probably has enough to do just getting used to her new surroundings. But she will soon start needing lots of things to look at and listen to.

When babies first learn to hold things, they like being given lots of different things to examine. However, they drop them very easily and don't know how to pick them up again.

Once the baby can sit up, she will be able to play with toys more easily.

Once he can crawl, you can give him things that roll.

93

Babies in nature

Other babies are made, like people, by a mother and a father. In nature, when parents come together so that their sex cells can meet, it is called mating. The moment when the cells join together is called fertilization.

Animals

Animals have their babies in a very similar way to people. During mating, sperm swim towards eggs inside the mother's body. If sperm fertilize the eggs, babies grow in the mother's womb. They are born through her vagina and feed on her milk.

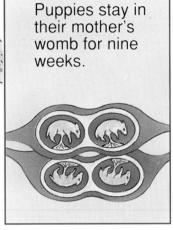

Puppies stay in their mother's womb for nine weeks.

Most animals have more than one baby at a time.

Birds

Baby birds grow outside their mother's body instead of inside. After mating, the mother bird lays her fertilized eggs. Babies grow in the eggs so long as the parents keep them warm by sitting on them.

A growing chick

The chick gets its food from the egg yolk.

Yolk

Air passes through the egg shell so the chick can breathe.

When the chick is ready to be born, it cracks open the egg shell with its beak and hatches out.

Eggs that we eat are unfertilized eggs. Chicks could not have grown in them.

Insects

Insects lay eggs after mating and fertilization. Most baby insects do not look much like their parents at first. They go through a big change before they are fully grown.

A caterpillar hatches from a butterfly's egg.

The caterpillar changes into a pupa.

The pupa becomes a butterfly.

Fish

Mother fish lay their eggs before they have been fertilized. The father then comes along and puts his sperm on them, and babies start to grow.

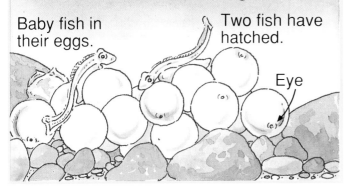

Baby fish in their eggs.

Two fish have hatched.

Eye

Caring for the babies

Animals and birds look after their babies until they can manage on their own. Baby insects and fish have to fend for themselves from the start.

Many animals carry their babies out of danger by picking them up in their mouths or giving them a piggy back.

Parent birds feed their babies when they see their brightly-coloured throats.

Babies snuggle up to their parents to keep warm.

Many animals keep their babies clean and show them affection by licking them.

Words and pictures puzzle

Can you remember the names of the things in these pictures? They are all in this part of the book. To help you, the names are on this page too, but each one is muddled up. Unmuddle the names and match them to the right pictures. Then look at the bottom of the page to check your answers.

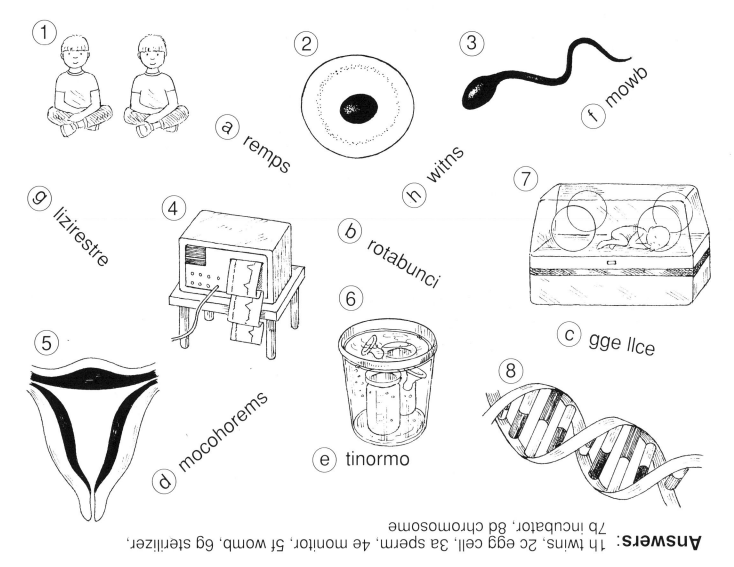

(1)

(2)

(3) ⓕ mowb

ⓐ remps

ⓗ witns

(7)

ⓖ lizirestre

(4)

ⓑ rotabunci

(6)

ⓒ gge llce

(5)

ⓓ mocohorems

ⓔ tinormo

(8)

Why Are People Different?

Contents

What is a person?

Have you ever wondered why you are what you are? Why are you the same as other people in so many ways, yet different too?

People everywhere are like they are for two main reasons. One is that they take after their parents. The other is that they are affected by the sort of life they live.

There are millions of different kinds of living things in the world.

What made you a person, not some other living thing like a cat or a daisy, are thousands of tiny things inside you called genes. People's genes are different from animal or plant genes.

Where you live

Your genes are only part of the story. You are the way you are also because of where you live: your surroundings. Another word for surroundings is environment. Your environment affects the way you live. This picture shows life in a part of West Africa.

These women are pounding vegetables called yams. They are made into a kind of porridge.

Young children stay close to their mothers.

This woman is carrying pots.

You got, or inherited, your genes from your parents.

Your parents inherited their genes from their parents.

Genes are the instructions which make your body work in the way it does. Everyone gets their genes from their parents, at the moment when they start to grow inside their mother.

Some things about you, like the way you look, depend a lot on your genes.

People all look different because of their genes.

Although everybody has genes, they are arranged in a different pattern in different people. That is one of the reasons why one person is not quite like another.

Overhanging thatch keeps rain off the walls.

Houses are made of mud bricks which have been dried in the sun. They are nice and cool inside

The weather is hot. Long, loose cotton clothes help people keep cool.

Oven

One big family

Everyone everywhere is really part of the same huge family which scientists call humans or human beings.

Everyone's bodies and brains are all made in the same way.

Where did people come from?

Jellyfish have been around for hundreds of millions of years; people for only about two million.

Creatures which were a bit like small apes lived about 10 million years ago.

There have not always been people in the world. There were plants and animals long before any humans. So where did people come from?

Most scientists think that living things gradually change, or evolve, over a very long time. They think people evolved from ape-like creatures.*

Out of Africa

Experts think that the first people evolved in Africa. They think they gradually spread all over the world from there, in the directions of the arrows on this map.

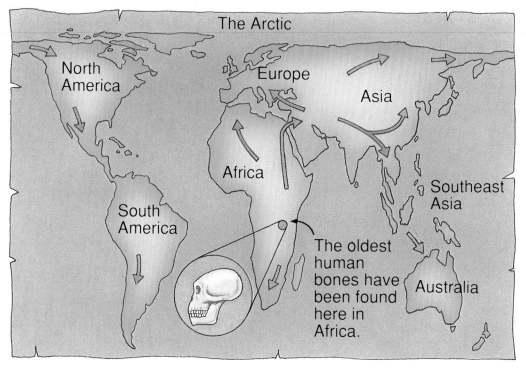

The Arctic

North America

Europe

Asia

Africa

Southeast Asia

South America

The oldest human bones have been found here in Africa.

Australia

100   *Some people do not believe things evolve. They believe God created people as they are today.

The first people

Stone

Stick

Humans had evolved by two million years ago. They walked on two legs and had hands which could use tools. They hunted animals and gathered wild plant foods.

Chimps

Young humans are very much like young chimps.

The animals people are most like today are chimps. Nine out of every ten human genes are almost the same as chimp genes. The main difference is that people are brainier.

Your oldest relations

The first people whose bodies and brains were like yours evolved about a hundred thousand years ago. They made many weapons and tools, and could probably talk. This picture shows life in a cool place.

These people hunted with spears.

They lived in caves and in shelters made from animal skins.

They made fires: for warmth, for cooking and to frighten off wild animals.

They sewed animal skins to wear.

Taking after your parents

The genes you get from your parents control the way your body lives, works and grows. The picture below shows just a few of the things about you that depend on your genes.

The way you live cannot change your genes. It can affect how your body copes with some genes though.

Your hair: whether it is dark or fair, curly or straight.

Your eye colour

Your face

Your skin colour

Your voice

Some people seem to inherit genes which make them more at risk of tooth decay than others.

If they do not eat much sweet food and clean their teeth very thoroughly, their teeth may stay healthy.

How genes work

Most things about you are decided by several genes. A few, such as hair and eye colour, depend mainly on one gene from each parent. The example on the right will give you an idea of how genes work.

Your hair colour depends on the mixture of your two hair colour genes. A dark hair gene is dominant (strong). It blocks out genes for other colours. A fair hair gene blocks out a red hair gene.

Jessica's mother has a dark and a red hair gene. Her dark gene blocks out her red.

Jessica's father has a fair and a red hair gene. His fair gene blocks out his red.

Jessica happened to inherit both her mother's and father's red hair genes.

Where are your genes?

Your body is made of millions of tiny living parts called cells. Your genes are stored in your cells, on special threads called chromosomes.

Chromosome —

Cell

Your cells have 46 chromosomes each: 23 from your mother, 23 from your father.

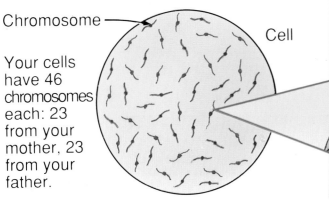

Chromosomes are made of a chemical (DNA) which looks like a twisted ladder. There are hundreds of genes on each chromosome.

About 250 rungs on the ladder make one gene.

The rungs are arranged in a different order in different people. This is what makes everybody unique.

Exactly which of your parents' genes you get seems to be a matter of chance. That is why brothers and sisters do not always seem alike.

Only identical twins have exactly the same genes.

Genes or environment?

Simon walks with his feet turned out. Is this because of his genes or because he has copied his Dad? Nobody knows.

There is a lot that is still not known about genes. Nobody really knows whether some things about you depend mainly on your genes, your environment or both.

People and the weather

Living things evolve (change) to fit in with their environment. This is called adapting to the environment. Things that do not adapt, die.

Things that do adapt, survive and pass on their genes to their children. Gradually there come to be more and more of the well adapted things.

Woolly mammoths were well suited to life in the ice age. When the weather warmed up, they did not adapt and died out.

Humans evolved skilful hands and good brains. This makes them well adapted to their environment.

Body build

Over a very long time, people's genes have helped them adapt to the weather in different parts of the world. Groups of people have come to look different from one another because of this.

Plump people were better adapted to the cold. They survived and passed on their plumpness genes to their children.

The children passed on the genes to their children. Today nearly all Arctic people are plump.

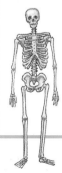

Slim people were not adapted to living in the frozen Arctic. They did not have enough body fat, which helps keep you warm.

Extra fat on the eyelids protects the eyes from the cold and glare of the snow.

Dark or fair skin?

In very sunny places people evolved dark skin. This blocks out some of the sun's harmful rays.

In cloudier places people did not need so much protection from the sun. They evolved fairer skin.

Dark skin helps protect people from too much sun.

People need some sunshine because it gives them vitamin D.

Ways of life

It is not only people's genes which have adapted to the weather. People have also adapted their way of life. Clothes, houses, even food and jobs can all depend on the weather.

Head-dress and veil give protection from the sun and wind of the Sahara Desert.

Houses are built on stilts in Southeast Asia, where there are often floods.

Living apart

Groups of people came to look different not only because of the weather but also because they lived far apart.

Most people used not to travel far, so they did not meet people from other parts of the world.

Today people from opposite sides of the world marry each other. Their genes get mixed together in their children.

Learning to fit in

Right from the time you are a baby, you have to start learning to fit in with the people around you. Different people have to learn to fit into very different kinds of worlds, depending on where they are growing up.

Showing the soles of your feet when you are sitting down is very impolite in Arab countries.

Eating in public places is impolite in Japan.

How you are expected to behave depends on your own family's way of thinking and on the general ways and rules of the place where you live.

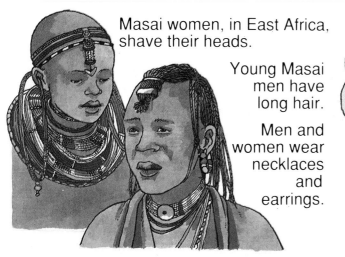

Masai women, in East Africa, shave their heads.

Young Masai men have long hair.

Men and women wear necklaces and earrings.

Someone who likes being outdoors may not much enjoy city life.

How you dress depends on what people in the place where you live think is suitable and attractive.

How happily people fit in depends on the kind of person they are and the type of environment they live in.

How do people learn?

Children learn how to behave by following the example of people they admire such as parents, teachers and friends.

Behaving well is sometimes rewarded by smiles, praise or even presents. This encourages someone to be good another time.

Babies

Young babies do not fit in all that well with other people. When they need something, they just cry for it. This is the only way they have of telling people something is wrong.

Babies cannot wait for things, or imagine how other people feel.

Children

As babies grow up, they learn to fit in, for example, eating at mealtimes, not just when they are hungry.

At school, you learn skills which will help you to cope with life in the wider world outside your family.

You also learn by playing with other children, for example, how to share and take turns in games.

Making a living

Everybody everywhere needs things like food and shelter. Most people have to earn money to meet their needs. The work people do depends largely on where they live and what kind of jobs there are in the area.

Farming

Most people in the world live in villages rather than towns and make their living by farming.

In some parts of the world machines are used.

Harvesting rice in the USA.

Harvesting rice in Southeast Asia.

In places where most people are farmers (Africa, Asia, South America) a lot of the work is still done by hand.

Farmers often have large families so there are plenty of people to help with the work, including the children.

Factory work

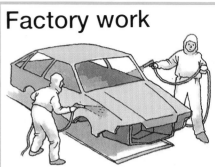

In places like Europe, North America, Japan and Australia there is a lot of industry. Many people work in factories, making things to be sold, or in offices. They get paid a wage.

People in industrial places often live in small families. They may move to find work.

In some places farmers do not get paid but keep some of what they grow.

108

Herding animals

In a few places, where it is too dry to do much else, some people herd animals for their living. They have to keep moving from place to place to find water and grazing land for the animals. These people are called nomads. They get most of what they need from their animals.

These people in Central Asia live in felt tents. (Felt is made from animals' wool.)

The tents are warm, and can be taken down and moved fairly easily.

The people keep sheep, goats, yaks, horses and camels. They sell animals to buy things they need such as wheat.

From the animals they get meat, milk and cheese; and wool and skins to make into clothes, tents and blankets.

They use the animals for getting around.

Fishing

Some people by the sea depend on fishing for their living, especially in places where there is no farming or industry nearby.

In the Arctic it is too cold for crops to grow. This man is fishing through a hole in the ice.

Other jobs

Some jobs are done all over the world, for example, teaching, nursing, or office work. Others are only done in certain places.

Tea will only grow on hills in warm wet places. It is grown in India and China.

Picking tea

109

Talking to each other

There are thousands of different languages spoken in the world today. The language with most speakers is Chinese. In second place is English.

How did language begin?

People gradually began to give meanings to the sounds they made.

Nobody is sure when or how people started to talk. They may have begun with noises such as grunts, and signs such as pointing.

Borrowing words

As people move around the world, their language goes with them. Words from one language often creep into another. Below are just a few words which have come into English from other languages:

potato (Native American), *anorak* (Inuit), *tea* (Chinese), *jungle* (Hindi), *garage* (French), *pyjamas* (Urdu), *orange* (Arabic), *robot* (Czech), *coach* (Hungarian).

Body language

In Indonesia it is rude to point with your finger. People use their thumb.

You do not only talk in words. You also use your face and body. Some things, like laughing and crying, mean the same everywhere. Some do not.

Language families

Many languages are related. French, Spanish and Italian all evolved from Latin, the language of the Ancient Romans. English is similar to German and Dutch.

Learning to talk

By the time they are one, most babies can speak a few words and understand many more.

Bedtime Joe

Babies' babblings include all the sounds it is possible for the human voice to make.

No

Bah dee moo

Young children gradually learn to speak the same language as their parents just by hearing and copying the sounds they make.

Same but different

The same language is often spoken differently in different places.

Hello *Hi* *G'day*

United Kingdom   U.S.A.   Australia

Even the same person can speak differently in different situations. Do you talk the same way to your friends as you do to your teachers?

Writing

There are over 50 different alphabets. Most West European languages have used the Roman alphabet since the time the Romans ruled the area. On the right are some letters from different alphabets.

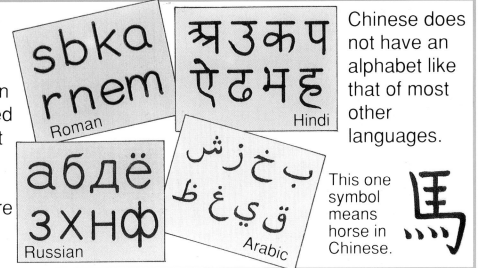

sbka rnem
Roman

अ उ क प
ऐ द म ह
Hindi

абдё
зхнф
Russian

ب خ ز ش
ظ غ ي ق
Arabic

Chinese does not have an alphabet like that of most other languages.

This one symbol means horse in Chinese.

馬

Moving around

Right from the time the first people moved out of Africa, groups of people have left one area and gone to settle in another. Journeys made long ago help to explain why people live where they do now.

Hunger

Sometimes people move because their crops die through drought (lack of rain), floods or disease.

In Ireland the potato crop failed in 1845 and people were starving. Thousands left for America or England.

Where from?

As people move around, they take their ideas and the things they use with them. Here are a few examples of where things started out.

Guinea pigs Potatoes }	South America
Fireworks Ice cream }	China
Arithmetic Oranges }	The Middle East

Slavery

In the 1600s and 1700s, millions of Africans were forced to go to America and work as slaves in the fields where sugar, tobacco and cotton were grown.

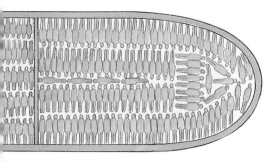

The slaves were packed like sardines on ships for the journey. Many died.

Plan of a slave ship.

Jobs

People often move from the countryside into towns to find work. Sometimes they move to a completely foreign country, often one which has close links with their own.

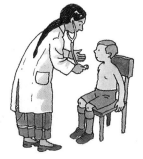

In the 1950s, many doctors moved from India to Britain, where more doctors were needed.

Power

There have been many times when one group of people has moved in on another and tried to rule them.

In the 1500s, Spain conquered many parts of South and Central America and ruled them for years.

Spanish is still spoken in those countries (shown yellow on this map), making it the third most spoken language in the world.

Brazil (Portuguese spoken here.)

Land

Sometimes people have moved to find new land to live on and farm. This has often led to trouble.

In the 1800s, many Europeans went to North America. There were fierce battles as they tried to take land there.

European settlers

The Native Americans were pushed into living only in certain areas called reservations.

Native Americans

Disagreements

Sometimes people are badly treated just because of what they believe or even who they are. This often happens in wartime.

Many Jews fled from Central and Eastern Europe at the time of World War II to escape being killed.

Prisoners

In 1788, the British government began sending prisoners far from home to Australia as a punishment.

Many stayed and made their living in Australia when their time in prison was over.

113

What people believe

People's beliefs depend a lot on what their families believe and on the religion and ideas that are taught in the place where they grow up. There are many different religions. Some have a lot in common.

The Japanese Shinto religion teaches that gods are in nature.

People pray at places like this.

Many religions involve believing in some kind of god or gods. Believers may pray to their god, often asking for help or giving praise and thanks.

Religions try to explain how the world and people were made. It is only fairly recently that scientists have figured out the idea that living things evolved.*

The Christian and Jewish religions teach that God made the world and the first man and woman: Adam and Eve.

Festivals

This Muslim is going from door to door, collecting rice for the poor.

Religions give rules for how to behave. For example, Muslims are expected to give to the poor and old.

Noisy processions are meant to frighten away evil spirits.

Chinese New Year is celebrated near the end of winter and welcomes in the spring.

Festivals usually celebrate special events, often religious ones. They may celebrate an important stage in a person's life: getting married, for example. They may celebrate an event in nature, such as a good harvest.

Many religions involve believing in some kind of life after death. Hinduism, for example, teaches that people are reborn into the world. If you are good in this life, your next life will be a better one.

Hindu holy men give up their possessions and try to live a good and simple life.

Politics

People with different political ideas disagree about the best way to organize and rule a country.

Greens believe it is all-important to improve the environment before it is ruined totally.

In some places people have no say in who rules them. In most countries elections are held. Then people can vote for those they think will run the country best.

Voting in India

115

People in groups

People everywhere are much more alike than they are different. However, it is sometimes interesting to think about people as different groups.

Male and female

Without the bodily differences between men and women, human beings would soon die out because no babies would be made.

What makes the difference between a boy and a girl is just one chromosome out of the 46 you have in each cell in your body.

Ethnic groups

People of the same ethnic group have relations who lived in the same part of the world long ago. They often share the same language, customs and beliefs.

People whose relations originally came from Britain often eat British Christmas dinner in Australia.

The way men and women behave differently and do different tasks has a lot to do with where they live and how they were brought up.

In Bali, Southeast Asia, women do the heavy work on building sites.

Many crane drivers in Dutch ports are women.

Friends

Friends may be quite different in some ways.

People may become friends because they have similar hobbies, interests or ideas; or just because they like each other. Friends often help each other.

Young people

Young people* are learning to manage without their parents. They often go around in groups; this gives them a feeling of belonging while being free of their families.

Old people

Old people may not be as fit as they once were but the things they have learned during their long life can be very interesting and useful to younger people.

Countries

People living in the same country live under the same government and have to obey its laws. Laws vary from one country to another.

ALCOHOL FORBIDDEN IN THIS COUNTRY

Alcoholic drink is banned in some countries.

Disabled people

Disabled people cannot easily do some of the things most people take for granted. There are different types of disability. Some can be overcome.

A wheelchair marathon

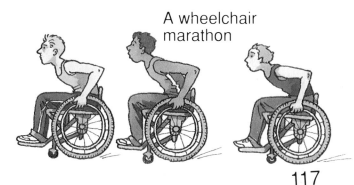

*To find out about children, see page 107.

One world

Humans have always had to adapt to survive and still need to adapt today. The main challenge now is for people to change their way of life before they damage the environment so much that they can no longer live in it. Here are some of the things humans can do to improve their environment.

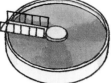
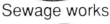

Sewage works

Clean sewage (waste from toilets and drains) properly so it does not pollute rivers and seas. Half the people in the world do not have clean, safe drinking water.

Find new kinds of energy which do not pollute the air people breathe. (Machines need energy to work.)

Wind turbines like this can be used to make electricity, without pollution.

Stop dumping harmful chemical waste from factories, farms and even homes in rivers and seas.

Make things from materials which do not harm the environment when thrown away. Better still, make them from materials which can be re-used.

Bottle bank

Rare orchid

Stop letting wild animals and plants die out. Besides being important in themselves, some may be useful to humans as new types of food or medicine.

Use better farming methods which do not damage the soil.

Stop cutting down forests. This destroys the homes of animals and plants, damages the soil and even causes changes in the weather.

118

Rich and poor

About a quarter of the people in the world own more than three-quarters of the world's wealth. Most people in the parts of the world shown green on this map are quite well off. Most people in the parts shown yellow are poor. Many people think that things should be shared out more fairly.

Some people in the world die from diseases caused by eating too much.

In the poorer parts of the world many people die every day from lack of food.

The future

Adapting will not be easy. It will take hard work and goodwill. People in rich countries do not always want to alter their comfortable way of life.

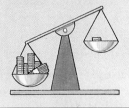

Leaving the car at home saves energy and reduces pollution.

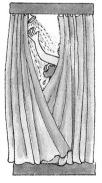

A shower wastes less water than a bath.

SAVE THE EARTH

Humans know what some of the problems are that face them. With the best brains of any living creature, they may well be able to find solutions.

Useful words

Ancestors

Relations who lived before you, from your grandparents back; relations from whom you are descended (see *Descendants* opposite).

Culture

The beliefs, customs (see below) and general way of life of a group of people.

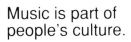

Music is part of people's culture.

Indian sitar

Custom

A habit, usual way of doing something, tradition.

It is a custom in many countries to take a present to a birthday party.

Descendants

The children, grandchildren, great grandchildren, and so on, of someone. You are a descendant of your parents, grandparents and so on back.

Queen Elizabeth II is a descendant of Queen Victoria.

Environment

Everything that surrounds a living thing and affects its life. Your environment includes the area where you live, your home, school, family, friends and possessions.

Inherit

1 To have passed on to you in your genes by your parents and ancestors.

He inherited his grandad's curly hair.

2 To be left something by someone when they die, for example, money or gold rings.

Index